UNION WORK

A Manual for Local, County, District,
and State Christian Endeavor Unions

By

Amos R. Wells

Editoral Secretary of the United
Society of Christian Endeavor

First Fruits Press
Wilmore, Kentucky
c2015

Union work: a manual for local, county, district, and state Christian Endeavor Unions, by Amos R. Wells.

First Fruits Press, ©2015
Previously published: Boston and Chicago: United Society of Christian Endeavor, ©1916.

ISBN: 9781621714019 (print), 9781621714002 (digital)

Digital version at http://place.asburyseminary.edu/christianendeavorbooks/26/

First Fruits Press is a digital imprint of the Asbury Theological Seminary, B.L. Fisher Library. Asbury Theological Seminary is the legal owner of the material previously published by the Pentecostal Publishing Co. and reserves the right to release new editions of this material as well as new material produced by Asbury Theological Seminary. Its publications are available for noncommercial and educational uses, such as research, teaching and private study. First Fruits Press has licensed the digital version of this work under the Creative Commons Attribution Noncommercial 3.0 United States License. To view a copy of this license, visit http://creativecommons.org/licenses/by-nc/3.0/us/.

For all other uses, contact:

First Fruits Press
B.L. Fisher Library
Asbury Theological Seminary
204 N. Lexington Ave.
Wilmore, KY 40390
http://place.asburyseminary.edu/firstfruits

Wells, Amos R. (Amos Russel), 1862-1933.
    Union work : a manual for local, county, district, and state Christian Endeavor Unions / by Amos R. Wells.
    323 pages ; 21 cm.
    Wilmore, Ky. : First Fruits Press, ©2015.
    Includes index.
    Reprint. Previously published: Boston: United Society of Christian Endeavor, ©1916.
    ISBN: 9781621714019 (pbk.)
    1. United Society of Christian Endeavor. I. Title.
BV1426 .W57 2015

Cover design by Jonathan Ramsay

asburyseminary.edu
800.2ASBURY
204 North Lexington Avenue
Wilmore, Kentucky 40390

First Fruits
THE ACADEMIC OPEN PRESS OF ASBURY SEMINARY

First Fruits Press
The Academic Open Press of Asbury Theological Seminary
204 N. Lexington Ave., Wilmore, KY 40390
859-858-2236
first.fruits@asburyseminary.edu
asbury.to/firstfruits

UNION WORK

A Manual for Local, County, District, and State Christian Endeavor Unions

By
AMOS R. WELLS
*Editorial Secretary of the United Society
of Christian Endeavor*

BOSTON AND CHICAGO
United Society of Christian Endeavor

PREFACE

THIS book takes the place of " Our Unions " in the list of publications of the United Society of Christian Endeavor, but it is not a revision of that volume. " Union Work " is a new book from beginning to end, every sentence appearing here for the first time. Since " Our Unions " was written, twenty years ago, Christian Endeavor unions have obtained a remarkable development, calling for an entirely new manual. An indication of this development is the present volume, which, though strictly condensed, is three times as large as " Our Unions," and treats many important subjects which are not even mentioned in the former manual because they had not yet been introduced in union work.

It is hoped that many unions will form their officers and leading workers into classes for the study of this book under enthusiastic leaders. To facilitate this class work each chapter is followed by a set of questions upon it, with subjects for talks, essays, and debates.

It is the aim of this book to present a picture of Christian Endeavor unions in their manifold present-day activities, to set forth the methods of work that have been found most useful, and to make manifest the value of our unions to the societies, the churches, and the community. They train the Endeavorers in many modes of co-operation and in the management of large affairs, thus furnishing to the churches for their widest interests a splendid body of skilled workers. In most

3

communities they are the only interdenominational
agencies at work along many important lines, thus
drawing the churches together and doing much for the
uplift of their towns and cities. This book is dedicated
to the thousands of Christian Endeavor union officers
throughout the world, whose deep devotion and fine
ability are doing so much for the kingdom of God.
May they find in these pages not only practical directions for their tasks, but the inspiration for new zeal
and larger endeavors.

AMOS R. WELLS.

Boston, Massachusetts.

CONTENTS

5

CONTENTS

UNION WORK

CHAPTER I

HOW TO ORGANIZE A CHRISTIAN ENDEAVOR UNION

Where May Unions Be Organized?—It is often said, and said truly, that wherever there are two Christian Endeavor societies a Christian Endeavor union should be formed. Two societies, when co-operating in a union, can do far more than they could do separately. They will inspire each other to better work. They will teach each other all that each has learned about the best methods. They will be able to do much for the community, for their churches, and for the world that they could not do separately.

The union should include all the Christian Endeavor societies of the town or city, with the societies in the country round about that can attend meetings with the town societies, or that cannot more readily reach the meetings of any other union. Sometimes a country society may be nearer a city union belonging to another county than to the nearest city union of its own county, and it should join the union in the neighboring county. The new union will reach out as far as it can without trenching upon the proper territory of the nearest union. What this territory is should be determined by friendly consultation as soon as there is the least danger of overlapping.

7

Shall Any but Christian Endeavor Societies Be Admitted to the Union ?—This question is sure to arise at some time, if not immediately. The answer depends upon the local circumstances. It must be remembered that the fundamental purpose of the union is to promote Christian Endeavor work ; it is not to promote Christian fellowship in general, though that is an inevitable result of Christian Endeavor work, nor is it merely for social enjoyment. Therefore it must not take any societies whose aims are not harmonious with those of Christian Endeavor.

The new union must not include any society that is likely to prevent its being a Christian Endeavor union and promoting Christian Endeavor work. At the beginning of my own public Christian Endeavor work I was called to address a union in a city of considerable size. On my arrival I was told that I must not say anything about the Christian Endeavor pledge or anything else distinctively Christian Endeavor, for fear of offending a single society in the union which was not a Christian Endeavor society and whose denomination had its own separate young people's society. As was to have been expected, that union soon failed and ceased to exist. After some years it was revived as a Christian Endeavor union with none but Christian Endeavor societies, and has ever since been most prosperous, entertaining the State convention and carrying on a splendid work for Christ and the Church. This experience illustrates the conditions under which no society that is not Christian Endeavor in name as well as spirit should be allowed to join a Christian Endeavor union.

On the other hand, I myself as a union officer once advocated and voted for the inclusion in a union of a society which had been a thorough-going Christian Endeavor society, but, through the mistaken denominationalism of its pastor, had been transformed into a young people's society of the separatist type. The young people wished to remain in the union, and were thoroughly in sympathy with Christian Endeavor, as they had proved by years of fine service. They remained, and the union was none the less Christian Endeavor because of their presence. This illustrates conditions under which we may safely admit into our Christian Endeavor unions societies of other names. In every such instance, however, the union leaders may well talk earnestly with the pastor of the society, and show him how his society can be just as loyal to its denomination if it has the interdenominational name as if it shut itself up with the denominational one. Urge upon him the duty of strengthening a great movement which has done more perhaps than any other to promote real Christian union; and it could never have done it with a multiplicity of names and a lot of separate organizations.

Who Should Organize the Union?—The near-by Christian Endeavor union may well discover a chance for service in forming a new union. Its officers can speak from their own experience of the advantages of a union and the work it can do. Or, the union may be suggested by any officer or member of a local Christian Endeavor society. This Endeavorer will talk up the matter, especially among the Christian Endeavor leaders and the pastors, and he may himself call the preliminary meeting. Some one Christian Endeavor society may start the union, calling upon the other societies to join in forming it. Some pastor, understanding the value of Christian Endeavor unions, may take the lead in forming one. Any one of these agencies, or all of them together, may make the move for a new Christian Endeavor union.

Consultations.—Whoever sets the ball to rolling, the new union should not be started without much consultation. All the presidents and other leading officers of the societies should be consulted, and all the Christian Endeavor pastors. Every one thus consulted is made to feel his importance, which is a pleasant feeling, and will henceforth be more interested in the union and realize a little better his responsibility for it. In this wide consultation you will probably meet with some objections, but it is far better to meet them at first and answer them than it is to allow them to come up later and clog the workings of the new union.

The Preliminary Meeting.—Having obtained the hearty approval of all these whom you have consulted, or at least of the large majority of them, you will call a preliminary meeting, which will include every Christian Endeavor pastor and all the officers of the Christian Endeavor societies of the community, counting in every society which you wish to have in the union, rural societies as well as town societies. Give them all a chance to become charter members.

At this meeting some one will describe fully the advantages to be gained from a Christian Endeavor union, and will answer questions about the workings of a union. After full discussion, the presiding officer will put the question, "How many are in favor of the formation of a Christian Endeavor union in this town?" The question being carried, the first step will be the appointing of two committees, one to draw up a temporary constitution, and the other to nominate a set of officers such as the temporary constitution calls for. These two committees will be appointed with great care. A committee will be chosen to nominate them, and this committee should be large and representative. After their report has been adopted by the meeting, it may adjourn.

The Tentative Constitution.—Of course the committee on the tentative constitution will do what it can to make it so good that it will become the permanent constitution, though, even if it does its best, circumstances are likely to arise making it necessary to change the constitution. But the committee will examine the constitutions of other unions, especially unions of about the size of the one to be formed, and in about the same circumstances. In general, simplicity is to be sought in a tentative constitution. Do not establish many departments at first. It is better to take up a few lines of work only, just the most important ones, and let the others develop slowly, as the workers become interested. Thus, for instance, if you have among the societies some one who is already interested in prison work and likely to become a good union leader in it, you might establish at once a prison-work committee; but otherwise you would not. You will, however, want all the usual officers, not forgetting the pastoral counsellor, and you will want a lookout committee, a conference committee, a social committee, a music committee, and a finance committee. Consult the officers of near-by unions as to the excellencies and defects of their constitutions, and try to profit by their advice.

The First Officers.—Much depends upon the nominations for the first set of officers. Indeed, if you cannot find a strong set of workers ready to take office in the new union, you would better not form it, but wait for a more propitious time. A union that has been long at work can endure poor leaders, though with difficulty; they would kill a new union at the very outset.

Very likely the nominating committee itself may contain much material for the first set of officers. If that is so, let no false modesty prevent the nomination of such persons, though they may well present to the meeting voting upon them a disclaimer of self-pushing. The union must be founded upon the spirit of self-sacrifice, if it is to endure.

The First Mass Meeting.—When these two committees are ready to report, you will summon all the members of all the Christian Endeavor societies in a mass meeting. Carefully fix upon an evening when they can all be there. Advertise it long in advance, so that you will have the evening clear. Make sure that all the Christian Endeavor pastors are present, if possible. Include all of them, if they are not too many, in the programme of the meeting for very brief speeches. It would be well to ask them to speak for one minute each on the advantages of a Christian Endeavor union, each dealing with only one advantage. The main address of the evening may be by some well-known Endeavorer, perhaps an officer of a prominent Christian Endeavor union. He will naturally tell about the various phases of union work as he has seen them developed, and will try to implant in the Endeavorers present a strong enthusiasm for co-operative Christian activity. Music will be provided in some variety, not by any means forgetting genuine Christian Endeavor congregational singing.

The chief object of the evening, however, for which plenty of time will be reserved, is the reading of the constitution and its full explanation, with answers of all questions that may be asked. You will vote upon it section by section, and then adopt the constitution as a whole. Following this you will present the nominations for the offices, and they will be voted upon. It will be as well under the circumstances to instruct the secretary of the meeting to cast one vote for the nominees. The meeting will close with the presentation of the president-elect and a few words by him, and with a brief prayer service asking for God's blessing upon the new undertaking.

The Importance of the First Months.—The first few months of a Christian Endeavor union do much to determine at least its first years. If it is started wisely and with zeal, it is sure to do splendid work. If it is started sluggishly and with poor plans, it will give the Endeavorers a distaste for union work that will be overcome with great difficulty. All concerned should therefore labor with much fervor and with constant prayer during the opening period of the union, and should determine that, so far as they are concerned, co-operative Christian Endeavor shall be firmly established in their community.

Where You May Make Mistakes.—The president of the new union will make a great mistake if he seeks to do it all, and does not work in all his officers. Failure to consult all who should be consulted, especially the pastoral counsellor, is another great mistake. Do not rely upon brilliant speakers in your first meetings, but, while you get as good speakers as you can, bring into every meeting many of the local workers. Do not rely for success upon the public meetings of the union, but make the union practically helpful to the societies in the conducting of their local work. Do not fail to advertise everything well—only be sure that you have something worth advertising. Begin and end all meetings sharply on time. Do not allow any plan to fail. Undertake few things—only what you are sure you can push through to complete success. If you do make failures—and you can hardly expect not to make any —learn from them all the lessons they have to teach you, and so organize successes out of them.

How to Insure Success.—Above all things, keep the union work upon the highest level of consecration. Carry on the union not to please yourself, but to please your divine Master. Form the most exalted ideals of union work, that it is to lead the societies to the fullest measure of Christian achievement possible for them. Keep these ideals always before yourself and before the societies, and allow no substitution of lower ideals. In other words, make it actually a Christian Endeavor union, a co-operative effort to do the will of Jesus Christ, and He will conduct it to a glorious and entire success.

Class Work on Chapter I

The Leader's Questions

Where may a Christian Endeavor union be profitably formed ?

Should a Christian Endeavor union contain any but Christian Endeavor societies ?

Who should organize a Christian Endeavor union ?

Who should be consulted before a new union is formed ?

What should be done at the preliminary meeting ?

What sort of constitution should be formed at first ?

Why should the first officers be chosen with great care ?

How should the first meeting of the union be managed ?

What are some of the mistakes to be guarded against in the first months of the new union ?

How can union success be insured ?

Topic for a Talk or Essay

The Advantages of Christian Endeavor Unions.

Subject for a Class Debate

Resolved, that Christian Endeavor unions should contain only Christian Endeavor societies.

CHAPTER II

THE UNION CONSTITUTION

Begin Simply.—When starting a Christian Endeavor union it is best not to frame an elaborate constitution containing probably much for which the union will have at first no use whatever, but to make the constitution very simple and add to it as the need for additions develops. Provide at first for only the ordinary officers and committees, unless you know that you will take up immediately some unusual line of work. Ordinarily at the start you will have enough to do merely to set going the customary union activities.

The following forms of constitution for the various unions, city, district, and State, are therefore only the outlines of constitutions, to be filled in by each union as its own growth suggests and requires. In many directions, however, the outlines here given hint at the enlargements that will later inevitably be made if the union progresses.

Suggested Constitution of a City or Local Christian Endeavor Union

Article I.—*Name*

This union shall be called the .... Christian Endeavor Union. [Note.—Local unions are generally named from the city or region which is their home, as the Chicago Christian Endeavor Union, the Merrimac

Valley Christian Endeavor Union; but other names may be used, such as the Clark Christian Endeavor Union, the Williston Christian Endeavor Union, the Golden Rule Christian Endeavor Union of such a city or region.]

ARTICLE II.— *Object*

The object of the union shall be to stimulate interest in societies of Christian Endeavor in .... and vicinity, to increase their number, to develop the mutual acquaintance of their members, to introduce the best methods of work, to serve the churches and the community in appropriate ways, and thus to make the Endeavorers more useful in the service of God.

ARTICLE III.—*Members*

Any society of Christian Endeavor connected with an evangelical church, mission, or public institution in .... and vicinity, whose constitution in its aims and prayer-meeting obligations conforms generally in spirit to the " Model Constitution," may join this union by notifying the secretary and upon approval of the executive committee.

ARTICLE IV.—*Officers*

The officers shall be a president, a vice-president, a secretary, and a treasurer, chosen from the active members of the societies composing the union. Their duties shall be those usually appertaining to these offices. [NOTE.—The pastoral counsellor, if the union has one, should be regarded as an officer of the union in the fullest sense. Other officers may be added as the union develops, such as a librarian, an assistant treasurer, an editor.]

ARTICLE V.—*Executive Committee*

The executive committee shall consist of the president, vice-president, secretary, treasurer, and the chairmen of the various standing committees of the union. This committee shall meet as a rule on the first .... of each month, and at other times at the call of the president, and shall plan for the best interests of the union, and as far as possible see that these plans are executed. Between the meetings of the congress the executive committee shall be empowered to transact business that requires immediate attention. [NOTE.—The pastoral counsellor and other officers that may be appointed by the union should be specified here. If the plan of a congress is not adopted, the presidents of the societies may be added to the executive committee, whose meetings will thus become essentially congress meetings.]

ARTICLE VI.—*The Congress*

1. A congress shall be constituted, consisting of the executive committee of the union and the president of each society in the union, with, if it is thought best, one other duly elected representative of each society. The congress shall discuss and transact the business of the union, and shall do its utmost to secure in every way the success of the union and of the individual societies.

2. Meetings of the congress shall be held once a month (or once in two months), and simple refreshments may be served if it is deemed best. [NOTE.—This section will be omitted, of course, if the functions of the congress devolve upon the executive committee; but in that case the executive committee should be enlarged as suggested above.]

Article VII.—*Lookout Committee*

A lookout committee shall be appointed, whose duty shall be to organize new societies wherever possible, to bring new societies into the union and introduce them to the work, and to encourage and help the weaker societies.

Article VIII.—*Pastors' Advisory Committee*

A pastors' advisory committee representing the different denominations in the union shall be appointed, before which all questions of importance which affect the life and work of the churches shall be laid. One of the pastors shall be selected as pastoral counsellor and elected for three years, and his name forwarded to the United Society of Christian Endeavor. [Note.—The pastoral counsellor may serve as a pastors' advisory committee of one, if it is thought best, with the proper changes in this section.]

Article IX.—*Other Committees*

Other committees shall be appointed, according to the needs of the union. They shall correspond, as far as is possible and wise, to the committees of the societies composing the union, and they shall, in every way possible, promote throughout the union the interests of the causes and committees which they represent. [Note.—Some unions prefer to designate these different lines of work as departments, and their heads as superintendents—missionary superintendent, citizenship superintendent, etc. In that case the suitable changes should be made throughout this constitution. After the union is well established, it will be best to give a section to each committee or department, defining its work, so that the constitution shall present a conspectus of the union activities.]

ARTICLE X.—*Reports*

Each committee shall report *in writing* at every regular meeting of the congress [or of the executive committee, if the union has no congress]. These reports shall be placed on file and preserved by the recording secretary in the archives of the union, thereby securing a history of its work. Once each year a summary of the work of all the committees shall be presented by the recording secretary to the union mass meeting. [NOTE.—It may be best for the chairmen of the committees to give reports to the union at the mass meetings.]

ARTICLE XI.— *Visitation*

As far as may be deemed necessary, and as often as is wise, each society of the union shall be visited by some member of the congress for encouragement and mutual help, and intervisitation among the societies shall be encouraged. [NOTE.—A definite scheme of visitation should be formulated, but generally it is better not to incorporate this in the constitution, as it is subject to change.]

ARTICLE XII.—*Elections*

A committee shall be appointed at the first meeting of the congress in each new year to nominate officers and chairmen of committees, which nominations shall, if deemed wise, be approved at the next meeting of the congress, and the nominees shall be elected at the first mass meeting of the union held thereafter. If the congress shall not approve the nominations, others shall be made by the nominating committee. The executive committee shall appoint the other members of each committee. [NOTE.—Each union must, of course, be the judge as to the best time for the election of officers. If the societies are in the habit of omitting their meetings to any considerable extent during the summer, it will be best to elect the officers just before the beginning of summer, so that the union may start off fully equipped and promptly in the fall.]

ARTICLE XIII.—*Mass Meetings*

Three or more mass meetings shall be held in the course of the year at convenient times. These shall be carefully planned by the congress, or a special committee of the congress, and such topics may be discussed within the scope of Christian Endeavor and such methods used to stimulate interest and attendance (such as banners, roll call, etc.) as may be deemed wise.

ARTICLE XIV.—*Finance*

The expenses of the union shall be met by any plans deemed wise by the executive committee and approved by the congress, but it is understood that no unnecessary expense shall be incurred.

ARTICLE XV.—*Conventions*

Interest in the State and national Christian Endeavor conventions shall be stimulated by the union. Information shall be given in advance, interest aroused, and when possible "echoes" of the convention shall be heard afterwards.

ARTICLE XVI.—*Amendments*

This constitution may be amended by a two-thirds vote of all the active members of the societies present at any regular meeting of the union, the amendment having been submitted in writing and notice having been given at least two weeks before action is taken. [NOTE.—The constitution should specify in what way the notice is to be given, as by letters to the corresponding secretaries of the societies, notice at a union meeting, or notice in the union paper, etc.]

Union Divisions.—Large city unions find it necessary to divide into sectional unions named from their localities, as the North Side Union, or given serial numbers, as the First District Union. Sometimes language divisions are necessary, as the German Union. The constitutions of these subdivisions of the union are like the foregoing in all essentials, while the constitution of the main or city union deals with the interests of the union as a whole. In this case the city union usually meets only once or twice a year, the divisional unions meeting more frequently. The union committees are found in each divisional union, the chairmen of each kind of committee constituting the main union committee on that subject. Each division has its own set of officers, the whole working with the central officers of the union.

A Suggested Constitution for District or County Christian Endeavor Unions

ARTICLE I.—*Name*

The name of this union shall be The .... Christian Endeavor Union.

ARTICLE II.—*Object*

The object of the union shall be to increase the number of societies of Christian Endeavor in this district, and to promote their efficiency as factors in Christian life and church work by bringing them into closer relation with one another through conventions, reports, and correspondence.

ARTICLE III.—*Members*

Any society of Christian Endeavor connected with an evangelical church or mission, or a public institution in this district, whose constitution, in its aims and in its prayer-meeting obligations, conforms substantially in spirit to what is known as " The Model Constitution," may join this union on its own vote to do so, communicated in writing to the secretary of this union, and approved by the executive committee of the union. The members of any society belonging to this union will be entitled to all its privileges.

ARTICLE IV.—*Officers and Committees*

The officers of this union shall be a president, three or more vice-presidents, a secretary, and a treasurer, whose duties shall be those usually belonging to such officers; also six directors, who, with the above officers, and the chairmen of all standing committees, shall constitute an executive committee, having charge of all business not otherwise provided for. The officers and directors shall be chosen at each annual conference, and shall begin their terms of service at the close of the conference at which they are elected.

Advisory Committee

The vice-presidents shall be pastors of different denominations, and shall constitute an advisory committee to which all difficult questions shall be submitted for advice.

Pastoral Counsellor

The union shall appoint a pastoral counsellor who shall serve for three years and whose name shall be sent to the United Society. [NOTE.—As the functions of the pastoral counsellor are the same as those of the ad-

visory committee, if you have the one you will not
have the other.   If the union has a pastoral counsellor,
therefore, it may have only one vice-president, who
will be chosen from the societies as is the president.
The pastoral counsellor should be a member of the
executive committee.]

Lookout Committee

There shall be a lookout committee of five members,
whose duty it shall be to see that wherever it is possible
a Young People's Society of Christian Endeavor is established and brought into the union.   This committee
shall also seek to establish Junior societies and Intermediate societies wherever needed, and shall do its
utmost to strengthen weaker societies as opportunity
offers.

Other Committees

The union may establish other committees as the
needs of the work suggest, and if these committees are
permanent their chairmen shall be members of the
union executive committee.

Article V.—Meetings

1.   The executive committee shall arrange the time,
place, and programme for an annual convention or
semi-annual conventions of this union each year.

2.   The executive committee may also provide for
meetings of a part of this union, at such place and time
as they deem best.

3.   The object of these meetings shall be instruction,
inspiration, and fellowship, and not legislation.   As
this union cannot be held responsible for the fellowship
of young people outside of the ranks of the Christian
Endeavor societies, and in order that the union may
not be used for partisan purposes, no delegates other

than those bearing fraternal greetings shall be appointed to other bodies, or received from other bodies.

ARTICLE VI.—*Finance*

The expenses of the union shall be met by the free-will offerings of the societies, and no tax or assessment shall be levied upon the members.

ARTICLE VII.—*Amendments*

This constitution may be amended by a two-thirds vote at any meeting of this union, provided notice of the proposed amendment is inserted in the call for that meeting, or is given at the previous meeting.

A Suggested Constitution for State Christian Endeavor Unions

ARTICLE I.—*Name*

The name of this union shall be The .... Christian Endeavor Union.

ARTICLE II.—*Object*

The object of the union shall be to stimulate an interest in Young People's Societies of Christian Endeavor and in unions of the same in this State, and to promote their efficiency as factors in Christian life and church work by bringing them into closer relationship with one another through conventions, conferences, reports, and correspondence.

ARTICLE III.—*Members*

Any society of Christian Endeavor, connected with an evangelical church, mission, or public institution in this State, whose constitution, in its aims and in its prayer-meeting obligations, conforms substantially in spirit to what is known as "The Model Constitution," may join this union on its own vote to do so, communicated in writing to the secretary of this union, and approved by its own executive committee. The members of any society belonging to this union will be entitled to all its privileges.

ARTICLE IV.—*Officers*

The officers of this union shall be a president, three (or more) vice-presidents, a secretary and a treasurer, whose duties shall be those usually belonging to such officers; also six directors who, with the above officers and the district secretaries and superintendents of departments, shall constitute an executive committee, having charge of all business not otherwise provided for. The officers and directors shall be chosen at each annual convention, and shall begin their terms of service at the close of the convention at which they are elected. At their first meeting they shall select superintendents for the different departments, such as Junior, Intermediate, Missionary, Citizenship, Quiet Hour, Tenth Legion, etc.

ARTICLE V.—*Meetings*

1. The executive committee shall arrange the time, place, and programme for an annual convention of this union.

2. The executive committee may also provide for meetings of a part of this union, under a call for a district convention at such place and time as they deem best.

3. The object of these meetings shall be instruction, inspiration, and fellowship, but not legislation. As this union is the servant of the churches and cannot be

held responsible for the fellowship of young people outside of the ranks of the Christian Endeavor societies, and in order that the union may not be used for partisan purposes, no delegates other than those bearing fraternal greetings shall be appointed to other bodies, or received from other bodies.

ARTICLE VI.—*Finance*

The expenses of the union shall be met by the freewill offerings of the societies, and no tax or assessment shall be levied upon the members.

ARTICLE VII.—*Districts*

The executive committee may divide the State into districts, and appoint over each a district secretary, whose duties shall be to assist in organizing new societies when called upon, to report such new societies to the State secretary, and do whatever he can to arouse and increase the interest in Christian Endeavor work.

ARTICLE VIII.—*Amendments*

This constitution may be amended by a two-thirds vote at any meeting of this union, provided notice of the proposed amendment is inserted in the call for that meeting, or is given at the previous meeting.

Class Work on Chapter II

The Leader's Questions

Why should we begin simply in making a union constitution ?

What kind of name is best for a union ?

What is the object of our union ?

What societies are eligible to membership in our union ?
What are our union officers ?
What are the duties of the executive committee ?
What is the union congress ?
What is the work of the union lookout committee ?
What is the work of the other union committees ?
What reports should the committees make ?
When are union elections held ?
What union mass meetings are required ?
How is the union financially supported ?
How may the constitution be amended ?
[Add questions covering other features of your constitution.]

Topic for a Talk or Essay

How to Make a Constitution Mean Much.

Subject for a Class Debate

Resolved, that a Christian Endeavor union is essential for success in local society work.

CHAPTER III

THE UNION PRESIDENT

The Importance of the President's Office.—The president of a Christian Endeavor union is faced with a great responsibility, and at the same time enjoys a great privilege. He is a leader to whom a multitude of young people look up with respect and affection. He can put large thoughts into their minds and can lead them out into large ways of service. If he is wise and strong and consecrated he can be a powerful influence for good in many lives and can do much for the cause of Christ through the Christian Endeavor societies.

The president of a Christian Endeavor union should be a young man (or young woman) of good executive ability, of thorough knowledge of Christian Endeavor, and of genuine consecration. He should have energy, good cheer, and abiding enthusiasm. He should be filled with zeal for the growth of the union in all helpful ways. If he has the right idea of his position and work, he will be eager to make good at the cost of all needed time and effort.

The President Presides.—Some presidents "do it all." They wish to seem to be "the whole thing." On the contrary, a wise president does nothing that he can get any one else to do for him. It is not his business to do things but to get them done. He is to preside over the doings of others, to inspire their activity and direct it. If a president does more than preside, that is a sign either that the union is in a bad way because of poor management in the past or that the president does not know what his true job is.

Inspiring His Fellow Officers.—The first work of the president is therefore to fill his fellow officers with his own zeal for Christian Endeavor and for the union. If the union has been going downhill, he is to fire them with determination to set it on the upgrade. The president should know about the work of each of his officers, so that he can put them to work and keep them at it. He will get them to adopt the best methods and will put them on the track of full information about their work. He will show each officer how important his task is and how much it means to the union. By making it plain how he leans upon them he will inspire them to do their very best.

Stimulating and Guiding the Committees.—The president should be *ex officio* a member of every committee of the union. He should be free to go to every committee meeting, and should be notified when the meetings are to be held. Of course, if the president is ignorant of the work of the committee and if he meddles with it officiously and not helpfully, he will not be a welcome visitor and the chairmen of the committees will not take pains to tell him when the committees meet; but if he takes pains to learn the best committee methods and plans and always has bright suggestions to make, if, moreover, he makes these suggestions quietly and modestly, the chairman and the committee will be glad of his presence.

If a committee does not get to work promptly at the beginning of the year, it is the business of the president to prod the chairman and set it to work. If a committee becomes lax during the year, it is the president's task to rouse it to renewed activity. The president must do this tactfully; but even if at last he has to take stern measures, it must be done. Personal feeling must not be allowed to stand in the way of the success of the entire union.

The Executive Committee.—The president will regard the meeting of the executive committee as the very heart of the union, and will spend much of his time in planning for this meeting and thinking up the best ideas to present to the members. The executive-committee meeting is the president's cabinet meeting. Here he meets, in effect, the entire union. Here he can lay his hand upon the moving forces of the union, and by a few words can do more than elsewhere he could do with much trouble. Suggestions and plans for the executive committee are given in the chapter on the subject. That chapter is for the president the most important in this book.

Visiting the Societies.—The president of a local union will visit the societies regularly and as often as he can. A visit from the union president will be counted an honor, and will do much to interest the society in the union. To emphasize the occasion, send word in advance that you are coming; but be sure to say that you do not want to make a speech, though you may take part in the meeting like the others. You want to have some idea of the condition of the society, and so you want to listen to the members, though of course you will say a few words to the society about the union as well as encourage them about their own work.

Be sure to have a talk with the pastor. Drop a word about the great advantage of Christian Endeavor to the church. Listen to him if he has any complaint to make about Christian Endeavor, and remove whatever misconception he may entertain. Praise him for his society, and ask for his influence on behalf of the union and his presence in the union meetings whenever practicable. Remain for the evening service if you possibly can. Talk privately with the most influential members of the society, and especially with those not already interested in the work of the union. Learn what you can about the best methods of the society, so that you may pass them on to other societies which you will visit. These visits of the president to the societies may be of the greatest benefit to the societies as well as to the union.

Conducting the Union Business Meetings.—The union business meetings are best held in connection with the union socials, if they are well attended, because nearly all present are Endeavorers, and you can give more time to these technical matters. If, however, it is necessary to conduct the business meeting in connection with the union mass meeting, with many present who are not Endeavorers, it will be wise to abbreviate the business as much as possible. Have it first and get it over promptly. Do not have long reports or many of them. Have them confined to matters of greatest interest to persons outside the union. Make it all run briskly, introducing as much fun and pointed earnestness as you can. Get it all done in fifteen minutes at the outside. The union business is important enough and interesting enough to the Endeavorers to warrant an entire evening given up to it, with the addition of a brief social and light refreshments.

The president will hold the meeting strictly to the subject before it. He will use tact in preventing disputes; and if any serious differences in opinion arise, he will suggest that the matter be debated in a committee and the conclusions given to the union later. He will have the matters which the meeting is to take up well arranged in advance as far as possible, and well thought out in his own mind. At the same time he will make it plain that any one is at liberty to introduce a matter of business, and that the union is to dispose of any matter as it sees fit without dictation from the board of officers. Welcome discussion, but keep it within proper bounds. Especially make sure that some large and worth-while plan is laid before every business meeting and adopted, so that the members will go away realizing that the union is doing things and that their attendance has been worth while.

Presiding over the Mass Meetings.—Some union presidents in presiding over the mass meetings make the great mistake of being too wordy. They seem to think that they are the principal speakers. Others are fussy and nervous, forgetting that serenity in a presiding officer promotes serenity and satisfaction in an audience. Others calmly throw away the programme, pay no heed to the times set for the various speakers, and embark upon an impromptu programme of their own quite heedless of the disastrous result, to the disgust of all present except themselves. Once I was the only speaker announced on the programme for the closing meeting of a State convention. The presiding officer called up this, that, and the other person from the audience—past presidents, leading ministers, and so on—and so occupied the time that it was ten o'clock before I was introduced. Most of the crowd had to get trains or trolleys, and I spoke to a procession. At another time I was present at a city union at which the only advertised speaker was a well-known clergy-man. The president of the union (also a minister of a large reputation) himself spoke for at least three-quarters of an hour, called upon several others to speak extemporaneously, got up an impromptu consecration meeting of three-quarters of an hour, and did not call upon the speaker of the evening till after ten o'clock. Said this speaker, " My train leaves in six minutes," and sat down. On another occasion I was the only speaker on the programme at the annual meeting of a large city union (one of the largest in the United States). Actually *twenty* speakers were introduced be-fore the president came to me, and again it was well past ten o'clock before I got my chance at that long-suffering audience. Such stories could be multiplied indefinitely. No exhortation is more needed by presi-dents than this, that they say little themselves, make that little as pointed and bright as possible, and devote themselves to keeping the meeting strictly on time.

The spirit of the presiding officer is largely that of the meeting, so that he should see to it that he is peace-ful, trustful, earnest, and ardent. If he expects a good meeting he will show that expectation in his whole bear-ing, and the audience will look for a good time with him.

In Touch with Other Unions.—Part of the duty of the union president is to become acquainted with the leaders of near-by unions and know what they are do-ing. He can do this partly by correspondence and partly by visiting the meetings of other unions and talking with the workers there. In both these ways he will gain many ideas which he will bring back with him to the executive-committee meeting of his own union. Visits to the executive-committee meetings of other unions will be particularly valuable to him, and he should invite the presidents of other unions to come to his own executive-committee meetings. Whenever he sees a chance for co-operation among the unions he should try to bring it about.

The President and the Larger Work.—Every union president should keep himself well informed regarding the work of the United Society of Christian Endeavor and of the societies all over the world. This can be done only by taking *The Christian Endeavor World*. Thus he will learn of the new printed helps which the United Society is constantly publishing and all the new plans for the societies and unions which it is constantly promulgating. It is no small part of the president's duties to see that his own union has its proper share in the world-wide plans of the United Society. If he can propose something to his union with the statement that all the other societies in the world are entering upon this good movement, he will be far more likely to obtain their hearty acquiescence.

The president will also keep his union at work upon some large plan for the good of the community, as is more fully suggested in another chapter of this book. He will also keep an eye upon the broad movements in the religious world, such as nation-wide evangelistic movements, or movements for more generous giving or for enlisting more men in the church work or for the banishment of the saloon. He will not do his duty till

he brings his union well abreast of these great mass
movements for the progress of the kingdom of God.

Defending the Union from Criticism.—The president of a Christian Endeavor union stands for the union
in the eyes of the community. If the union is attacked,
it is his business to reply to the attacks. If Christian
Endeavor is misrepresented, it is his business to state
the correct view of the matter. He can do this sometimes through the religious or secular papers, and sometimes by appearing before large and representative
bodies of men such as the ministers' meetings. If the
occasion requires it, he should not hesitate to ask for
such a hearing.

Advocating the Work of the Union.—The president
is not only the union's proper defender against criticism, but its advocate when it would appear before the
public asking for special support in its work. Sometimes this work is so large that the financial resources
of the union are not adequate, and thus the general
public must be called upon. The union may wish to
establish a public library or a gymnasium or a public
playground or a park. The president will take the lead
in such work, aided, of course, by the union committees
and backed by the pastoral counsellor and the ministers.

The State President.—The work of the president of
a county or district union is essentially the same as that
of a city union, but the president of a State union has
a somewhat different task. He cannot, of course, visit
all the societies, but he can visit most of the city or
county and district unions, and he can be at many of
their mass meetings and conventions. Whatever he

can do in thus becoming personally acquainted with the workers and stimulating them will add much to the success of the State union. He also must confine himself to the executive work that properly belongs to him, and must work through his officers, making much of the meetings of the State executive committee. These meetings will be held several times a year in different sections of the State, so as to be convenient to all the members of the executive committee in turn. It will generally be best to arrange with the city union to entertain the members of the State board, and in return they will be the speakers at a mass meeting of the union held in the evening. of their stay, the meeting of the executive committee being in the afternoon. Thus the State officers will have a chance to give the city a real stimulus in Christian Endeavor work.

Planning a Convention.—To the president belongs the initial work of planning the State convention, at least in its broad outlines. Often these outlines, however, will be presented to the State executive committee and thoroughly discussed with them, since fresh minds will be sure to suggest new and valuable ideas. The president may correspond with the speakers himself (he usually does) ; and whether he or the secretary does this, he should make sure that each speaker understands exactly what is expected of him as to theme and manner of treatment, and especially just how long a time he is to occupy and just when he is to come on. In planning the convention the president should remember that its aim should be the aiding of Christian Endeavor societies in their special work ; it is not a convention for Sunday-school work or for the discussion of current social problems or for political speeches or for sermons taken from last year's barrels, however eloquent the sermons may have been when given to their original audiences. Everything must be focused upon the actual needs of the societies, and be adapted to improving and stimulating Christian Endeavor work.

The president will not pack the programme so full that the interruptions and unexpected events will disturb it, but will leave a generous margin of time for these. He will make every session full of practical help for the Endeavorers. He will give them something to do in the sessions as well as much to receive. And upon it all, at every step, he will earnestly ask the blessing of the Holy Spirit.

The President Preparing a Convention.—Of course the president will work through a full set of convention committees. There will be committees on printing and advertising, on entertainment, on decorating, on music, on programme, on halls, on reception, on transportation, on press, on finance, on badges, on ushers, etc., but it is the president that must see that these committees are at work and that they keep at work actively and wisely. He will bring the chairmen of all the committees together in frequent meetings, will have reports from all committees, and will make sure at every step that good progress is being made. If the president does not live in the convention city he will be obliged to carry on much of this work by correspondence, but still he will often visit the convention city and consult in person with the workers.

The President Managing a Convention.—During the convention itself the president will keep his hand on all details of the work. He should be in telephonic touch with the heads of the different committees, arranging several times every day when they will report to him in person and receive suggestions from him. He will not always preside over the convention sessions, but will hand over part of this work to other officers of the union, never, however, giving it to any one that cannot do it well. He will especially make sure that the speakers are received cordially on their arrival, taken to their hotels or other places of entertainment, and brought to the convention building in time for their addresses. If possible he will look them up himself, and make sure that they fully understand when they are to speak and all other details. Through these multifarious labors the president must keep serene and cheerful, and be so happy himself that his happiness will overflow into the hearts of all the hundreds whom he has a most unusual opportunity to influence.

The President Training a Successor.—Every Elijah should train his Elisha. The president will not force any person upon the union as his successor, but he will not do his duty unless he so trains some one that he will make a good successor if the union sees fit to appoint him. If the president's work is well done, the union will doubtless be very glad to appoint him. This possible successor may usually be the vice-president ; but if the vice-president does not prove to be well fitted to the task, then the president will put some one else in training for it, getting him to help in the management of committees and leaning upon him in all the work of the union.

The President out of Office.—The privilege of working at the head of a Christian Endeavor union is so

great that it involves a life-long duty to keep in touch
with the work of the union and be ready to give it all
possible encouragement and aid. Many unions make
of past presidents members *ex officio* of the State executive committee, and thus wisely get the continued
advantage of their experience. Some unions have vet-
erans' associations, which the ex-presidents should certainly join. Ex-presidents will take a deep interest in
the work of their successors, praising them, cheering
them up, and giving them a hand of helpfulness whenever they can. They will attend the union meetings
whenever possible, and make it abundantly evident
that their heart is still in the work.

Class Work on Chapter III

The Leader's Questions

What kind of person should be chosen for a union
    president ?

What is the president's duty with reference to the
    other officers ?

What should the president do for the union commit-
    tees ?

What is the president's work in connection with the
    executive committee ?

What should the president do when he visits the socie-
    ties ?

How will the president conduct the union business
    meetings ?

How will the president preside over the union mass
    meetings ?

How will the president keep in touch with other unions ?

How will the president keep in touch with the larger work of Christian Endeavor ?

How will the president defend and advocate Christian Endeavor ?

How will the president prepare for a convention ?

How will the president keep a convention running well?

How will the president train his successor ?

How will the president help the work when out of office ?

Topic for a Talk or Essay

A President That Really Presides.

Subject for a Class Debate

Resolved, that humility is more necessary for a president than energy.

CHAPTER IV

THE UNION VICE-PRESIDENT

The Vice-President's Important Duties.—It is the fashion to think lightly of the vice-president and his work and regard him as a nonentity. This is a great mistake. Properly considered, he is one of the most necessary and important officers of the union. Few unions, however, make the right use of the vice-president, and indeed, few organizations of any kind.

The vice-president's one task, so far as most constitutions define it, is to preside in the absence of the president. But the president may never be absent; and then, since the vice-president is quite certain to be a person of ability, you have his powers left unused. Of course the vice-president must take the president's work in his absence, but how can he do it well unless he does part of the president's work, and a large part, when the president is not absent? In fact, the vice-president should be the assistant president of the union, always at the right hand of the president, ready to aid him in any task and taking off his shoulders as nearly half of his burden as is possible.

If this is done, the vice-president will be in training for the office of president and will be the logical successor to the president when he must give up that office. In some unions this is the regular and expected thing, though of course it should not be a hard-and-fast rule so as to bring about the election of an unfit person as president just because he has held the office of vice-president. This office is to serve as the testing out, and if the test is not passed successfully, you will look elsewhere for your next president.

Heading the Lookout Committee.—It is well to give the vice-president some definite work to do in the union at all times, and not merely when the president is absent. Perhaps the best task to assign him is to make him chairman of the union lookout committee. This is a post of great importance, and one that brings its occupant into touch with all the societies and with many phases of union work. Moreover, it is work of considerable difficulty, and if it is well done much of the president's care for the union will be lessened.

Overseeing the Committees.—In addition to the chairmanship of the union lookout committee, to which he may be assigned, *ex officio*, by the union constitution, the vice-president may well be asked by the president to look after a part of the other union committees and see that they are kept running efficiently, and the committees assigned him for oversight may be changed from time to time. Other branches of union work may be placed under his general superintendency as the need arises, such as the hospital work or the work for prisoners. In short, the president will call in the aid of the vice-president for every task for which he has no time or too little time, as well as for many tasks which the vice-president should take up merely to gain a more intimate knowledge of the union. And if the president does not of his own accord make this thorough use of the vice-president, that officer should feel no delicacy in at least offering himself for such services, though of course he cannot force himself into them.

Visiting the Societies.—The vice-president can always be free to visit the societies; and in this work, which is so important and arduous, he can greatly aid the president and benefit the union. The president and vice-president working together cannot visit the societies as often as they might be visited with profit. The vice-president will bring to the union executive-committee meetings the fruit of these visits in the knowledge of helpful methods discovered, and also in the experience of the needs of certain societies.

The Vice-President Presiding.—A wise president will not always preside over the meetings of the union executive committee or the mass meetings of the union, but will occasionally put his vice-president in his place. The vice-president may give him some excellent suggestions by the way in which he does things, and fresh methods of work are helpful even if they are no better than the old. The president will take this opportunity to sit in the audience and observe from that point of vantage how matters are going, or to sit in the executive committee and take part from the floor. This presiding of the vice-president's may be for a whole session or for only part of it; at first, certainly, for only part of the time.

A Vice-President's Conference.—The vice-president is usually not utilized in the societies as he should be, and to bring about this magnifying of his office the union vice-president may well call a conference of society vice-presidents early in their term of office. Obviously it would be well to have the society presidents there also! This larger view of the vice-president's work will be set forth, and the views of the presidents and vice-presidents regarding it will be heard and their questions will be discussed. In a society as well as in a union it is well to make the vice-president the *ex officio* chairman of the lookout committee.

The State Union Vice-President.—The work of the president of a larger union—county, district, or State — is so difficult that he needs the aid of his vice-president especially, and should avail himself of it to the full. Indeed, the State union usually has more than one vice-president, and the president will avail himself of the assistance of them all. Sometimes the various vice-presidents represent the different sections of the State, and are expected to superintend the work of the State union in their respective sections under the general direction of the State president. Sometimes the State union has a vice-president from each denomination that has Christian Endeavor societies in the State. These denominational vice-presidents are supposed to have oversight of the societies in their respective denominations, and to promote Christian Endeavor in their churches. They also will live in widely separated parts of the State, and will be of double service to the union and to the union president. They will be expected to look out for the interests of Christian Endeavor in the State denominational conferences, and to promote the cause through the various denominational papers.

The World's Union Vice-Presidents.—The World's Christian Endeavor Union has a vice-president in each of the States, and this officer will do for the president of the World's Union what the State vice-presidents do for the State presidents, and what the local-union vice-presidents do for the presidents of their smaller bodies. The World's Union has a great work to carry on for the mission lands of the world, where Christian Endeavor has not come to the period of self-support. Much money has to be raised every year for carrying on this work, and the vice-presidents may be of the greatest assistance in raising it. They will know how this money is spent—for the translation and printing of Christian Endeavor literature, for the sending out of Christian Endeavor organizers from Christian Endeavor lands, and for the support of native secretaries who promote the cause among their countrymen. The missionaries of all denominations are eager for this assistance, and are unanimous in their declaration that Christian Endeavor societies give them the greatest possible help in the training of the converts and the conducting of the native churches. All this work is done in each mission field under the close supervision and with the hearty co-operation of the missionaries of all denominations.

Class Work on Chapter IV

The Leader's Questions

Why is the vice-president an important officer ?

What are the duties of the vice-president ?

What committee work may be assigned to the vice-president ?

What work may the vice-president of the union do in the societies ?

When will the vice-president preside ?

What conference should the vice-president organize ?

What is the work of the State union vice-president ?
What is the work of the World's Union vice-president ?

Topic for a Talk or Essay

A Useful Vice-President.

Subject for a Class Debate

Resolved, that our union should have more than one
vice-president.

CHAPTER V

THE UNION SECRETARY

Corresponding and Recording.—Unions seldom have separate corresponding and recording secretaries, but one officer does both kinds of work. At the same time the union secretary is expected to do much that would be done by a printing committee, if a union had one, and by an advertising committee. If these committees exist, as they well may in a large union, some suggestions made below are for them and not for the secretary.

The Secretary's Records.—Of course the secretary will keep full records of all business transacted in the business meetings of the union, and also of the work of the executive committee. The minutes of the latter will be quite as important as those of the former. The secretary will take great care to record all motions passed, and in the very words of the motions. If you are in doubt, get the mover of the motion to write it out before it is passed, or read your own wording to the union, or the executive committee as the case may be. In addition to the motions passed, it will be useful for the secretary to record all important matters discussed, even when the decision is unfavorable. In later days it will be quite as useful to know that a certain plan has been considered and vetoed as to know that it was acted upon affirmatively.

48

Of course the secretary will not be able to write out the minutes during the progress of the business meeting, but will merely take very full notes. These notes should be written out as promptly as possible, before they have grown "cold," and should be copied into the permanent record book immediately after they have been approved at the next meeting. Procrastination on these two points renders the secretary well-nigh useless to the union.

Moreover, the secretary should be so familiar with the minutes of past meetings that he can turn to any former action with great quickness. It is a great drag on a meeting to be obliged to wait while the secretary fumbles over page after page, trying to discover what action was taken on a certain matter in a former meeting. To facilitate this reference to what has been done, the secretary should prepare a very full alphabetical index, and should keep it in the back of the record book. Bring it down to date with each new set of minutes.

The Union Scrap-book.—The recording secretary of the union should keep a union scrap-book. It will be a large volume, ample for the accumulations of years. In it the secretary will paste, in careful chronological order, all the printed matter published by the union. There will be the programmes of the union meetings, the blanks that may be issued for statistics, printed notices sent to the societies, and all the printed matter which the different union committees may issue, as far as the secretary can obtain copies.

The secretary will give frequent notice to all the officers and chairmen of his desire to have copies of whatever is printed, that they may thus be preserved. Date everything in the scrap-book, and write neat titles if the material is not self-explanatory. Whatever is printed about the union may well be included, even the newspaper accounts of the union meetings, though here the secretary will duplicate the work of the press committee, which also will keep a scrap-book; but that will be for its own use and the use of its successors, while the union scrap-book will have a wider use. The union scrap-book may also contain copies of all the important and interesting printed matter issued by the individual societies.

If the union is a large one, a series of scrap-books would be more useful, one for each important class of matter preserved. The recording secretary will keep this scrap-book where all union workers can have ready access to it, and will remember that its usefulness is much less if it is not kept promptly up to date.

The Secretary's Reports to the Union.—The secretary may duplicate parts of the reports of other officers and some of the committees, but this should be avoided if possible. The report will be read at the union business meeting. It will contain a summary of the most important actions of the executive committee. It will briefly review the last union meeting. It will tell about the prominent union activities, unless these are covered in the reports of committees. And, most important of all, it will picture the present state of the union, giving the totals of all statistics that the secretary has been able to gather. If the executive committee has recommendations to make to the union, they will properly come through the secretary's report.

All of this will be as bright and as brief as the secretary can possibly make it. Let the report be an event, a genuine contribution to the value and interest of the meeting. It will be, if the secretary has original ideas and an original way of expressing them, even though the report is confined to the work of others.

The Secretary's Notifications.—The secretary, having access to the official minutes, is the one to notify all persons instructed by them to undertake any duty. If committees are appointed, he will notify the members in writing, and at once. It makes no difference that some of them may have been present when the action was taken; the written notification should be sent as a reminder. The chairman of the committee should be told that he is the chairman. If a new society has been received into the union, the secretary of that society (the corresponding secretary) should receive written word to that effect, together with a cordial greeting. The president of the union may well sign this communication with the secretary. If the union business meeting or executive committee has taken any action regarding the work of any officer or committee, this action should be communicated in writing by the secretary.

It is the duty of the secretary to send written or telephonic notices of all meetings of the executive committee; and these notices should be sent well in advance, that plans may be made.

Sometimes it is best for the president to correspond with the speakers of the union meetings; but if he wishes help in this direction, the secretary should give it. Always, if the president has obtained the speakers, it is well for the secretary to write to them as a reminder when the time for the meeting draws near, sending them copies of the printed programme and giving them all necessary instructions as to the meeting place and the time of speaking.

The Printing of the Programmes.—If there is no printing committee, it is the duty of the secretary to see to the printing of the union programmes. The president will give him the material, unless, indeed, he has himself done the corresponding with the speakers. He will consult the president as to the arrangement of the programme, which is thus a joint product. Poor printing never pays. The programme should be so neat, accurate, and attractive that it will be a good advertisement for Christian Endeavor, though extravagance should, of course, be avoided.

The Union Constitution.—The secretary will superintend the printing of the union constitution and by-laws, the fundamental union documents. Enough copies should be printed to supply every active member of the union for several years to come. A slight charge may be made for the copies, to cover the cost of printing. It adds much to the interest which the members will take in the union to see that each member has a copy of the constitution and is familiar with it.

The Union Statistics.—It is the duty of the secretary to collect the statistics of the union. What these shall be will be determined by the executive committee, and the different chairmen will call for the facts most needed in their work. The secretary will ask the societies to tell how many active, associate, and honorary members each has, what committees, what is the average attendance, how much money is given for missions, how many Endeavorers united with the church, how many copies are taken of the local or State Christian Endeavor paper and *The Christian Endeavor World*, how many members teach in the Sunday school, how many are church officers, the average society attendance on the regular church services, and any new or especially interesting kind of work which the society has taken up. Of course other items may be called for, or some of these may be dropped, as the wishes of the executive committee may decide.

A Secretaries' Conference.—The union secretary may well hold, at least once a year, at the opening of the society year, a conference of all the recording and corresponding secretaries in the union. At this conference the union secretary may give a little talk on the work of the secretary in general. Then he will call upon a recording secretary and a corresponding secretary previously appointed, who will talk about the duties of their respective offices. Finally there will be a general question-box on the work. The union secretary will take this opportunity to spur the corresponding secretaries to greater faithfulness in their work, especially in the furnishing of the statistics desired by the unions.

Union Maps.—One device which the secretary may adopt for placing before the societies the facts he gathers is a union map. This will show the bounds of the union and the principal geographical features. It will indicate all the churches, and will distinguish with a gilt star each church that has a Christian Endeavor society (Young People's); also with a red star each Junior society, with a blue star each Intermediate society, etc. This map will show at a glance the field of the union, and the parts of the field that are not yet cultivated.

Helping the President.—The secretary, like the vice-president, will be one of the president's best helpers, and will take up portions of the president's work as he is asked to do so from time to time. He will be especially useful in visiting the societies and learning the needs and special excellences of each.

The Secretary a Reference Bureau.—The union secretary should learn the very best Christian Endeavor methods and have them at his tongue's end. He should openly invite questions from the societies regarding the work, and should be so faithful when the questions come that they will come in ever-increasing numbers. This he can bring about only through the most careful study of the best Christian Endeavor helps published by the United Society.

The Secretary's Correspondence.—The union secretary may wisely carry on a correspondence with the secretaries of other unions, for the purpose of learning their best methods of work in the societies as well as the unions. From this correspondence he may prepare what he will call "suggestion sheets"—budgets of Christian Endeavor plans, briefly stated, that will be helpful to the societies of his union. These budgets will be printed on some duplicator, and sent to the corresponding secretaries of the societies for them to communicate to their fellow members.

Especially will the union secretary be prompt in answering the letters of the State secretary and the general secretary of the United Society of Christian

Endeavor, since failure to respond promptly here means hindrance to very important affairs.

The State Secretary.—The duties of the secretaries of county and district unions are much like those of the local-union secretary, but the State secretary has a wider field. He will do for the State executive committee what the local-union secretary does for the executive committee of his union. He will do for the unions of the State what the union secretary does for the societies that constitute his union. The statistics gathered by the State secretary will be determined largely by the State officers. Much of these statistics will be brought together by the local unions and simply forwarded to the State secretary. He cannot use the telephone and face-to-face conversation as spurs to attention to his requests for information, but he must use "follow-up" letters. Some State secretaries have been driven to the necessity of telegraphing delinquent societies in order to make their statistics complete, but usually a persistent bombardment of letters will accomplish the feat. Once a secretary is waked up, he is likely to remain wide-awake.

In the State convention the secretary is the president's right-hand man. To him may be assigned the supervision of some of the local committees and of certain details of the convention. He will see that the speakers are on hand, aiding the vice-president in this work. He is often the time-keeper, and should hold each speaker strictly to the time allotted him, making sure at the outset that the speaker understands what that time is and just how he is to be notified when the time has nearly expired. He will make the convention announcements, giving a ruling from the State executive committee as to what announcements to bar. For example, purely personal announcements, as that Miss Jones would like to meet Miss Smith at the west door after the session, should not be made, but only those that plainly belong to the convention or have some urgency attaching to them. All these legitimate notices should be given in a strong, penetrating voice that is easily heard throughout the hall. I have seen more than one convention whose success was assured more by the good humor and tact and the businesslike firmness of the secretary than by any other factor.

Class Work on Chapter V

The Leader's Questions

Distinguish between the corresponding and recording secretary.
What will the secretary put into his records ?
What will the union scrap-book contain ?
What will the secretary put into his reports ?
What notifications will the secretary make ?
What printing will the secretary see to ?
What statistics will the secretary collect ?
What conference will the secretary conduct ?
In what other ways will the secretary help the union ?
What are the duties of a State secretary ?

Topic for a Talk or Essay

The Secretary's Trials and Triumphs.

Subject for a Class Debate

Resolved, that our union should have both a recording and a corresponding secretary.

CHAPTER VI

THE FIELD SECRETARY

The Importance of the Office.—The field secretary is the only salaried officer of our Christian Endeavor unions, and that fact indicates his importance. He alone gives his full time to the work. He continues in service year after year, while the presidents and all other officers serve for only a short time. He comes to have great influence over the State. The Endeavorers know him better than they know any other officer. They trust him and love him. It is essential, therefore, that the field secretary be chosen with the greatest care, and that he be very faithful to his great task.

Qualifications of the Field Secretary.—Thus far, at least, only the State unions have employed field secretaries. The field secretary, therefore, should be some one of State size, some one of a large-calibre mind, able to cover a big territory in his plans and in his labors. Of course he must be a man of high ideals and of pure life, wholly consecrated to the Lord's work and deeply in love with Christian Endeavor. He should be without fads, either in thought or in method. He should be sympathetic and tactful, able to work with others and lead others. If he have a bright humor, so much the better. He should be a good talker, and, if possible, also a good writer. He should be a man of unflagging industry and of good common sense. In money matters he should be practical and strictly honest, keep-

ing every cent of the union funds sacredly apart from
his own. These qualities are not easy to find in one
person, but they have been found many times in the
splendid corps of field secretaries set to work in our
State Christian Endeavor unions.

Working with Other Officers.—Since the field secretary must work in close co-operation with the other
officers of the State union, and especially with the State
president, secretary, and treasurer, it is necessary that
he shall be able to work with others, deferring to their
judgment though making his own opinions felt, and
laboring in a brotherly spirit, not seeking to push himself forward but seeking solely the good of the cause.
He will be loyal to the State union, and will lay all his
important plans before the State executive committee,
first having gained the assent of the president. He
will not try to " run " the State union, but will regard
himself as an executive officer to carry out the plans
which the State officers jointly decide upon. Any
suspicion of self-seeking and of ambition would spoil
his influence and ruin his work.

The Field Secretary and the Department Heads.—
The field secretary, with his wide view over the State
and over all the work of the State union, will sometimes find it difficult to sympathize with the feeling of
the department heads. Each very naturally thinks of
his department as the one thing to be pushed. Each is
so deeply interested in his work that he wants a big
appropriation for it and much attention given to it. It
will be hard for the field secretary to satisfy all these
superintendents when each wishes him to advance his
bit of the work with all his time and strength. But
the path for the field secretary will be marked out by

a sincere interest in each department, an interest as sincere as that felt by the head of the department, though not so absorbing. Not once in his meetings and correspondence will the field secretary forget any department of the State work, but will advocate each as opportunity offers, and will make opportunity for each whenever he can. Do something practical and outstanding for each department during the year, so that you can point to at least one evident piece of co-operation with it. Often consult with the department heads, seek their advice, find out what they are doing, and show them that your purpose is to aid them in every possible way, consistently with your responsi-bilities for the rest of the work and workers.

Aiding the Unions.—Much of the field secretary's work will be done through the local, county, and dis-trict unions, and he will be in closest touch with their officers. He will visit the unions periodically, and come to know them intimately. He will study the weakness of each, and try tactfully to remedy it. He will also learn the strong points of each, and tell the other unions about them so that they may be imitated. He will get the union officers into the habit of bring-ing to him their perplexities, and will do his best to solve them. He will help in the obtaining of speakers and the planning of programmes. He will introduce new and helpful departments and lines of work, and will communicate to the union officers all particularly helpful methods about which he may learn. As he visits the unions he will arrange whenever he can for a personal conference with all the union officers in ad-dition to the public meetings.

The Field Secretary's Journeys.—Of course the field

secretary must be a great traveller. He will probably spend more time "on the road" than in his office. Personal contact with the Christian Endeavor leaders in all the towns and cities is what will accomplish most. He will be present, if possible, at all the Christian Endeavor conventions held in the State, and it will be well to arrange that the conventions in one part of the State shall all be held on days close together, so as to avoid expense in travelling. This is to the advantage of the unions, as thus they will be able to use many speakers in partnership. Always when he travels the field secretary will try to cover as many appointments as possible on the way, and thus keep down expenses.

Raising His Own Salary.—Sometimes the field secretary is expected to raise a large part of his own salary, if not all of it. This is not the ideal condition, for the salary should be raised by the State treasurer, but sometimes a field secretary can be employed under no other conditions. It is better that all the money raised by the field secretary should go to the State union for its work in general, including, of course, the work of the field secretary.

The field secretary may take collections for the State work at all his meetings. Some field secretaries are able to raise money by giving entertainments or lectures. The best way is for the State treasurer to get direct pledges from the societies and unions for the State work, but the field secretary can do much to help transform these pledges into money. The banner plan is best. According to this plan the State union expenses are apportioned among the county unions in proportion to the number of societies in each county, and the "banner counties" are those that raise this assessment for the current year.

The Field Secretary's Correspondence.—Half of his work the field secretary will do in meetings of various kinds, and the other half he will do by correspondence. He must be a vigorous and effective letter-writer, in touch with the workers all over the State, getting from them their best plans, sympathizing with them in their troubles, ready to try to help them out of their perplexities. His letters will aim to make them regard him as a personal friend. He will be prompt in replying to his correspondents, and his first task on returning from a journey will be to answer letters. If his journey is a long one, he should arrange to have his mail forwarded to some place where it will be sure to reach him, so that he can reply from there to the more pressing communications. A traveller's typewriter would be a good investment for a State union.

Arousing Interest in the State Union.—Wherever the field secretary goes he will talk up the State Christian Endeavor union—to local-union workers, to pastors, to business men, to society officers. He will try to impart to every one the same enthusiasm for the State union and its work that he himself has. He will talk up the work of the different departments, and show why State-wide co-operation is necessary. He will have the history of the State union at his tongue's end, and will know all about the State constitution. Especially he will be able to show that the State union helps the local unions and the local societies, for that is why the State union exists, and by proving this he will do most to inspire zeal for the State union. A little folder, summarizing brightly what the State union is and does, will be of the greatest assistance to him.

State Christian Endeavor Campaigns.—The State union cannot do everything at once, but it will take up, one after another, the most important items of Christian Endeavor progress, and will try to advance those movements among the unions and societies. It may be a campaign for new members or for new societies. It may be an efficiency movement, or a campaign for soul-winning, or for increasing missionary gifts through the Tenth Legion, or bettering private devotion through the Quiet Hour. Whatever the campaign is, the field secretary will be the leader in promoting it. He will introduce it in all his addresses. He will slip leaflets about it into all his letters. Where-ever he goes, he will set the societies and unions to working along the lines of the campaign. He will gather accounts of results as fast as he can, and print them for the stimulation of the workers. At the close of the campaign have some sort of celebration. These campaigns are of the greatest value, unifying the efforts of the workers all over the State and putting many to work that would not otherwise do anything.

Arousing Interest in the State Convention.—As soon as any plans for the State convention have been made, and that should be as soon as the last convention is over, the field secretary will get busy stirring up interest in the coming gathering. Convention clubs will be formed among prospective delegates. Little articles will be written for the papers. Circulars and posters will be sent to the societies. Information will be obtained about the principal speakers and scattered broadcast. The pride of the unions will be aroused, each seeking to have the largest representation. As the field secretary goes about from one point to another over the State, he will talk convention with so much fervor that soon the Endeavorers will be looking forward to it as one of the greatest events of their lives, which it may well prove to be. Much of the success of the State convention depends upon this hearty preliminary work of the field secretary.

The State Paper.—Generally the field secretary, who is more closely in touch with the work and the workers than any other officer of the State union, edits and publishes the State paper. His many journeys give him ample news material, and he gets a lot more from his correspondence. The paper gives him the best opportunity to push the State work of all kinds. He will insert helpful items regarding all the departments of the State union, but it is best not to assign space regularly to any one, since nothing makes a paper more uninteresting than material written because one has space to fill and not because one has something to say. The State paper should be a newspaper pure and simple, full of snap, written in brief and pointed paragraphs, and published at a low price so that every Endeavorer may subscribe. Some field secretaries have earned their whole salaries from the subscriptions and advertisements of the State paper they conducted.

The United Society of Christian Endeavor.—The field secretary can be of the greatest assistance to the United Society of Christian Endeavor by passing on to the unions and societies the United Society publications and the ideas and suggestions of the national officers. He will be in the closest touch with the United Society, will carry samples of the latest helps, and will try to introduce them everywhere. In this work he will aid the societies and unions even more than the United Society. He will give the United Society officers the benefit of his experience, suggesting improvements in the helps they publish and new kinds of helps that may be called for by his constituency. The United Society depends largely for its effectiveness upon the State and local unions, and there is no better bond between the two than the field secretary.

The Field Secretary's Difficulties.—Often the field secretary has to make a place for himself, especially if no such work has been done in his State or if it has been intermitted for some time. As he is the only salaried officer of the union, much will be expected of him, perhaps more than is reasonable. He may be obliged, in order to make his own work effective, to criticise the work of some other officer, perhaps the president or the treasurer or the secretary. It may be necessary for him to transform some departments, introducing better methods, and this necessity may get him disliked for a time. He will make these changes tactfully though firmly, and will manifest so clearly his own unselfish purpose that soon all his fellow officers will join him in eager zeal for the best.

The Field Secretary's Rewards.—The work of the field secretary is hard. I would advise no one to enter upon it who wants to get through life without difficulties. But it is a task full of romance, full of inspiration, and crowned with rich rewards. The field secretary has a chance to enter helpfully into the lives of thousands of young people. He can turn many of them to the gospel ministry or to missionary service. He can set in motion a wave of evangelism that will sweep many souls into the kingdom. He can encourage a host of weary workers. He can fill thousands with a holy ambition. He can be the means under God of transforming many lives, and he can become one of the most powerful factors for good in all his State. His rewards will be abundant in the gratitude of his fellow Endeavorers, in their love for him and friendship that will last through all his life, and, best of all, in the joy and approval of his Master, Jesus Christ.

Class Work on Chapter VI

The Leader's Questions

Why is the field secretary an important officer?
What are his qualifications?
How should he work with the other officers?
How will he aid the unions?
How will he plan his journeys?
How may he help raise his own salary?
How will he arouse interest in the State union?
What Christian Endeavor campaigns may he conduct?
How will he arouse interest in the State convention?
What is his relation to the State paper?
What is his relation to the United Society of Christian Endeavor?
What are some of the field secretary's difficulties?
What are the field secretary's rewards?

Topic for a Talk or Essay

Experiences of Some Field Secretaries.

Subject for a Class Debate

Resolved, that a field secretary should not raise his own salary.

CHAPTER VII

UNION FINANCES

Why Unions Need Money.—Our Christian Endeavor unions do not need much money. They have no salaried officers (except that some State unions have field secretaries devoting their whole time to the work, and therefore paid salaries), and their expenses are very little. Indeed, it would be hard, if not impossible, to find an institution accomplishing so much with so little money as a Christian Endeavor union.

But our unions do need some money. They need money for printing the programmes and notices of meetings, the constitutions and other union documents; they need money for the expenses of an occasional speaker, for postage, for music if there is a union chorus, for free reading-matter used to advance the work. If the union is doing some local missionary or philanthropic work, such as conducting a fresh-air home or work for sailors or prisoners, money will be needed in generous amounts for this also.

The Educative Value of Money-Raising.—The money-raising side of union work is not to be scorned. It is the best possible training for the money-raising on a large scale that some of the Endeavorers will be called upon to do for their communities and for the denominations. This money-raising is an art, involving many principles of business and much knowledge of human nature. If the financial work of our Christian Endeavor unions trains the young people in this art, the churches should be deeply grateful.

No Dues or Assessments.—Since this work is to be educative, it is essential that it shall be based upon the right principles ; and the basis of successful money-raising for the kingdom of God is the arousing of deep personal interest in the object for which the money is to be raised. No arbitrary methods, such as the levying of dues or assessments, will answer this great end. They are easy methods, but very fallacious. The gifts must be voluntary. They must be born of loyalty to the work and a sincere desire for its advancement. Thus only will the giving become permanent and take care of itself, except as the zeal of new members is to be awakened.

For the same reason the rivalry of societies, upon which so much stress is sometimes laid, is a false principle of money-raising. Even if the rivalry is always good-natured, it is not the best motive, and money-raising thus conducted is not educative for the larger work of money-raising for the kingdom of God to which the Endeavorers will later be called. On the contrary, whatever advertises the work of the union and interests the Endeavorers in it is a legitimate adjunct to the work of the union treasurer.

The Union Treasurer.—It follows from all this that the union treasurer should be some one with thoughts far above dollars and cents. Of course he should be a good accountant, honest as the day and accurate to a cent. He should keep the union money strictly separate from his own, and should bank it properly. He should pay it out only on properly signed orders, and should insist upon signatures to vouchers for every cent thus paid out. He should always have his accounts thoroughly audited for his own protection, even if the union does not insist upon it—and a union always should insist upon it.

But far beyond these elementary requirements, the union treasurer must believe fervently in the work of the union and be able to communicate that fervor of belief to others. He will not talk up the union finances but the union work, how necessary it is and how blessed are its results. In proportion as he succeeds will the Endeavorers give to the union treasury—and he will not even need to ask them!

The Union Finance Committee.—No one man can properly do the work of the treasurer of a Christian Endeavor union. There should be a finance committee, partly to assist the treasurer and partly to serve as an example to the societies, for in each one of them the treasurer should be aided by a finance committee. The union finance committee should consist of one person from each society if the union is small, or from each section of the city if the union is large. These members will represent the financial work in their own societies or localities, and the task thus divided will be easily done. At the same time the training which the work of treasurer affords will be given to more persons, and a successor to the treasurer will be readily found when he must retire.

The Union Budget.—Every union treasurer and his finance committee will prepare a budget at the opening of the union year, not only because this is the right way to raise union funds, but for the sake of setting an example to the societies, which also should have budgets, and because this is the right course for all similar Christian organizations. The budget will be formed after careful consultation with the union officers and committee chairmen, and it will be approved by the union executive committee before it is passed on to the societies. It will state how much money should be raised in the union during the year and will divide this sum among the different departments of the union work, so that the members of the union can see at a glance just what the money is to be used for.

Moreover, attached to the budget will be a rough estimate of the proportion of each society, which is easily found by dividing the total sum by the number of societies in the union. There must, however, be also some allowance for the size of each society and the ability of the members to pay. Divide the total to be raised by the number of members of the union, and state how much, on an average, each member must pay if the sum is to be raised. Each society can readily see what is its proportion by multiplying this sum by the number of its members. This, however, is only a rough approximation, since some members are able to pay many times as much as other members, and the society should be reminded of this and told that societies and members should give according to their ability and desire for the work, merely using these estimates as rough guides, and not in any sense as assessments or dues.

Money-Raising Devices.—While no plan is better than the plan just suggested—that of a clearly-set-forth budget, toward which the societies contribute, each according to its ability, some unions prefer methods more direct and immediate. Some rely upon collections made at the union mass meetings. These are well enough, but they are very uncertain, and they levy the expenses of the union upon those only that attend the union meetings. They lack the educative value that attaches to the other method. Some treasurers prefer to go before the union meetings and present the work of the union, calling for pledges to be made on the spot by representatives of the societies there present. Sometimes blackboards are marked off in squares, each square representing five dollars of the sum to be raised. As each five dollars is subscribed, a square is filled in with colored chalk. The method is graphic, and the exercise may be made interesting and even exciting to the members. It may answer for occasional use, and especially for raising money for unusual purposes, but it soon wears out if adopted regularly. Its chief value is for emergencies.

Union Entertainments.—Some large city unions raise all the money needed for their work by means of annual union excursions, either boat rides or railroad trips. Others have union picnics with charges attached, or union field days for athletic sports with admission charges. Sometimes unions raise considerable sums by means of cantatas or pageants, or other pleasant and profitable entertainments. These all have a social value and are worth while in themselves. They may be made to advance the union work in other ways besides helping, at least, to provide funds. While it is seldom that they can wisely take the place of the definite budget and an educative campaign to interest the Endeavorers directly in the work of the union and its support, yet they are worth while as an adjunct to that more dignified and permanent method.

Frequent Reports.—The union treasurer should make frequent and regular reports as to the condition of the treasury, and should not allow the union finances to fall behind without notifying all concerned. To this end among many others a union printed bulletin is a good thing. Many unions have gone into debt printing elaborate and costly papers, unnecessarily large and chiefly designed to gratify the ambition of some would-be editor or publisher. So far as I have knowledge, no city union, not even the largest, has made a financial success of a Christian Endeavor paper, and very many have incurred thereby heavy debts which have crippled them financially for years. No union has a constituency large enough to support a paper containing comments on the prayer-meeting topics, general Christian Endeavor articles on methods, Christian Endeavor stories, and church news. On the other hand, most unions could wisely get out modest bulletins, perhaps four pages each, and published monthly. These would be of inestimable advantage to the union as a medium for advertising the meetings and the work of the union officers and committees and for aiding the treasurer in his money-raising campaign. Such a bulletin would contain advertisements which might pay for it, and it should have a very low subscription price. Its articles should be bright and brief, and should bear particularly, every one of them, on the union work. The treasurer and finance committee might well start such a bulletin, though it should be managed by a separate editorial committee made up of the brightest writers in the union.

A Conference of Christian Endeavor Financiers.— The union treasurer should hold early in the union year a conference of all the society treasurers, including the members of the society finance committees so far as they have been appointed. Of course the members of the union finance committee will be present.

The conference will discuss in all its phases the question of the raising of money for the support of the union and of the local societies and for the missionary gifts of the societies. These conferences will be very practical, and will lead to definite money-raising campaigns in the societies and throughout the union. A later conference may well be held for reports of progress and for solving the difficulties which the workers may meet.

County and State Union Treasurers.—The work of these officers is so similar to that of the local-union treasurer that a separate description is not necessary. In these larger unions finance committees are positively needed, and the budget system is here a necessity. The same methods of raising money are wise in all kinds of Christian Endeavor unions. The same regard must be had for the inspiration of zeal for the union, and in them all money-raising must be based upon the love for the work that is implanted in the hearts of the Endeavorers.

The Salaries of Field Secretaries.—The work of the field secretary who gives his entire time to the State union is so helpful and vital that it justifies the payment of a living salary, even though this greatly increases the financial necessities of the union. Sometimes the field secretary raises his own salary largely by collections taken at his meetings. This, however, is a heavy handicap upon his work and limits his usefulness, so that the collections he may make should be regarded as merely incidental and the union should not rely upon them for his salary any more than is strictly necessary. Some field secretaries have made the State Christian Endeavor paper pay a part or even all of their salaries, but these are very exceptional instances. Too often the State paper is an expense to the State rather than an asset. It should be regarded more as a medium of communication, and a very useful one, than as a means of money-raising.

Convention Money-Raising.—Some State treasurers notify the societies in advance of the State convention how much money will be needed by the State union during the coming year, and ask that their delegates be authorized to pledge the societies at the convention for generous sums, or the proportion of each society may be stated. Then a part of a convention session is devoted to the raising of the funds for the year, or the work may be done quietly by the collecting of written pledges in the course of the convention. In any event the societies should have before them a definite statement of how much money will be needed by each department during the coming year—a well-planned budget.

Some State treasurers have obtained fine results from the recognition of counties or districts that have come up to their apportionments as "banner counties," to which banners are awarded, either literally or figuratively. A State paper is almost a necessity if a "banner" campaign is to be carried on.

Combination of Appeals.—It confuses and displeases societies and especially their pastors if separate appeals are made during the year by the local union, the county or district union, and the State union. The treasurers of all these unions should work together. The State union should raise its money through the counties and districts, and the latter should raise their money through the local unions, where they exist.

Thus each local union will place in its budget a certain sum for the county union, and each county union will place in its budget a certain sum for the State union, so that the local societies will make only one gift to a union, and that will be the local union. This plan calls for the closest co-operation among the unions and for the formation of plans and the making of budgets very early in the church year ; but both the co-operation and the promptness are great gains from every point of view. Moreover, they furnish still another element in the education of our young people for the great work of money-raising for the kingdom of God to which some of them, and perhaps many of them, will be called after they have completed their training in Christian Endeavor.

Class Work on Chapter VII

The Leader's Questions

Why do unions need money ?

Why may it not be raised by dues or assessments ?

What kind of person should the union treasurer be ?

What is the work of the finance committee ?

What is a union budget ?

What are some good ways of raising union money ?

What reports should the treasurer make ?

What conference should he conduct ?

What points are to be noted in the finances of the larger unions ?

Topic for a Talk or Essay

The Educative Value of Money-Raising.

Subject for a Class Debate

Resolved, that the union should encourage the practice of tithe-paying.

CHAPTER VIII

THE UNION EXECUTIVE COMMITTEE

The Heart of the Union.—A good executive committee with regular and enthusiastic meetings always means an active and successful Christian Endeavor union. And the converse is true: a weak and inactive executive committee, with meetings few, irregular, and spiritless, always means a feeble union, doing little and doing that little in a lifeless way.

This is because the executive committee brings together the heads of the union work, all the heads. Its meetings give an opportunity for that consultation which is the life of all business. If the president of a union tries to do everything, he will fail miserably. The very essence of Christian Endeavor is co-operation. "Everybody is wiser than anybody." Our Christian Endeavor prayer meetings are successful because each member contributes a little. Our unions will be successful on the same principle. If the union president looks well to his executive-committee meeting, he need not fear for the rest of the union work.

How Large Should the Executive Committee Be?— The ideal union executive committee will consist, in the first place, of all the officers of the union, and of the chairmen of all the union committees or department superintendents. This will make a sufficiently large committee for the transaction of business.

75

Usually, however, the executive committee may well add to its membership the presidents of all the societies in the union. They will greatly strengthen the executive committee, and at once put it into the closest possible touch with the societies. If this would make the executive committee unwieldy, then the presidents must be reached in some other way. The success of most of the union undertakings depends upon reaching the societies with the union plans, and they can best be reached through the presidents. We need not fear executive committees of considerable size, especially if the plans for executive-committee meetings suggested below are carried out. Some of them require numbers for enthusiasm and effectiveness. Moreover, it must not be forgotten that the actual work of the union is done by the committees of the union, and that the executive-committee meetings are for deliberation and decision regarding the large outlines of the work. Therefore, on the whole, I favor the inclusion of the society presidents in the executive committee, at least for the regular meetings of the committee, while power may be given to the president and his cabinet of officers to take quick action on details between the meetings of the full committee, if such action is found necessary.

Time and Place of the Meetings.—It is best that the union executive committee should have a regular time for its meetings, and the time in most cases should be once a month, on whatever day is most convenient, say the first Monday evening. Nothing should be allowed to prevent the meeting. Whoever must be absent, even if half the members are away, let the rest gather and talk over the affairs of the union. Impress upon the members of the committee the importance of their work and the necessity for regular attendance if the union is to prosper. Urge them to set down the date as a previous engagement, taking precedence of all other engagements. Follow up every absence as carefully as an absence from the consecration meeting in a local society.

And if a regular time is advantageous, so is a regular place. The place should be central, and always available. The president's home is a good place, if it has a room large enough. Some unions rent a room for the meeting-place. Some central church may have a room that will be given up to the committee on its regular evenings. If a meeting-place and a meeting-time can be set apart for a series of years and for one administration after another, attendance will become more and more a habit and the union will gain much from this persistency.

The Essentials of a Good Executive-Committee Meeting.—The first element of every executive-committee meeting, after the opening devotional service, should be reports from all the officers and committee chairmen, telling what has been done during the past month, and especially what progress has been made on the new plan formed for the officer or committee at the last meeting. Next will come a period devoted to general questions, every one being free to bring up any problem or preplexity that has arisen in the course of the work. The third portion of the time will be spent in deciding upon some one plan for each officer and committee to work upon during the coming month. It may be the continuance of the plan adopted at the previous meeting, if that plan has not been completely carried out and it seems best to continue it ; otherwise it will be a brand-new plan. The president will have a suggestion ready perhaps for every officer and committee, in case the officer or committee has nothing ready to suggest. He will ask also for proposals from the main body of the committee. The plan that seems best will be adopted. This definite fixing upon some fresh line of work for each officer and committee is very important, and should be insisted upon. In proportion as it is thoroughly and wisely done is the union likely to advance in usefulness and power. Next may come the consideration of the general condition of the union, briefly set forth by the president or the chairman of the union lookout committee, followed by suggestions from the other members. And finally some very earnest prayers will be offered, asking for the blessing of the Master upon the work undertaken in His name. It will be seen that an executive-committee meeting having these elements cannot fail to be a real power in a Christian Endeavor union, leading it to genuine service and to increasing strength.

The Executive-Committee Supper.—It will be very much easier for the young business men to attend the meetings of the executive committee if they can go right from their business and take supper with the committee. At the table the affairs of the union will be discussed informally, and the business will be in good shape for rapid transaction after supper. The pleasant social intercourse brings the members of the committee very closely together, and they soon become firm friends. The plan has so many advantages that it has been adopted by a number of unions, in spite of the trouble involved. Sometimes the supper is at some restaurant where a room is regularly set apart for the committee and the supper is all ready for them on the appointed nights.   Sometimes the society of a centrally located church gets up the supper and makes a slight profit from it.   Sometimes an inexpensive hotel is patronized.

Speakers at the Executive-Committee Meetings.— It is well to give éclat to the meetings of the executive committee by having some good speaker talk on a general subject connected with the work—some principle of Christian Endeavor or some important form of Christian service appropriate to the union.   The speaker will be some one who recognizes the value of such an important body of young workers, though they are comparatively few in number, and is glad to set his thoughts before a group that will be eager and able to carry them out.

If it is not feasible to obtain such a speaker, you may have a general discussion of some large principle or line of work, several members of the committee being prepared to start the discussion and lead it to a helpful conclusion.   If it works out well, the discussion may furnish a theme for a union mass meeting and possibly may supply some of the speakers.

The Executive Committee and the Union Mass Meetings.—This leads us to speak of the relation between the executive committee and the general plans for the mass meetings of the union.   The president will lay before the committee his central idea for the coming meeting before he makes a complete programme or obtains any speakers, and he will receive many valuable suggestions as to both ; perhaps, indeed, some theme will be proposed that will be substituted for the subject he had in mind.   If the planning for the mass meeting

becomes a one-man affair, the audience also is likely
to become a one-man affair!

Special Meetings of the Executive Committee.—
Sometimes, in order to bring a certain society or a certain part of the city into closer touch with the work of
the union, it will be best to hold a special meeting of
the committee in a place quite distant from the usual
place.   The time may be the usual time, but even this
may need to be changed.   The local society will furnish a simple supper for the committee, and the business of the committee will be transacted during the
meal and immediately after it.   Then the evening will
be filled with a public meeting in the main auditorium
of the church.   This meeting will be well advertised,
and will be addressed by the ablest speakers in the
executive committee.   They will talk about Christian
Endeavor in general, and the work of the union in
particular.   They will introduce many facts and will
put the whole as brightly as possible, so that the meeting will be an attractive advertisement of our society
and its work and a general inspiration to Christian Endeavor in that church.

**Christian Endeavor Literature at the Executive-
Committee Meetings.**—Some unions have made a great
success of the executive-committee meetings in the
matter of the introduction of the latest and best Christian Endeavor helps.   A committee of the union or its
secretary obtains these helps from the United Society
as they are issued, and they are attractively exhibited
during the meeting, with the result that the members
of the societies present take them away and introduce
them in turn into their own societies.   This is a great

advantage to the United Society, and an advantage
equally great to the local work.

**The Pastoral Counsellor in the Executive Commit-
tee.**—We have said that every union officer should be
present at the meetings of the executive committee.
This applies especially to the pastoral counsellor, who
should be urged to be present as often as is consistent
with his many duties as a pastor. Indeed, the choice
of a pastoral counsellor will be determined largely by
his ability to go to the executive-committee meetings
with a fair degree of regularity, since in no other way
can he gain a thorough knowledge of the aims and
methods of union work. No important plan will be
adopted without his advice and approval, representing
the advice and approval of the pastors and the churches.

A Unifying Plan.—Often the welfare of the union
requires that it should unify its workers by the adoption of some large task which will draw them all together and compel them to do their best. This task,
of course, will respond to some pressing need of the
community, or the Endeavorers will not be zealous for
it and obtain the support of the community in it. It
may be proposed by the president or some other officer,
or it may grow out of the work of one of the union
committees. Whatever it is, labor upon it will fuse
the union into a vigorous whole, and make it far easier
to win new triumphs in the future.

The Executive Committee in the Societies.—If the
work of the executive committee is to amount to anything, it must go down into the societies and win the
support and co-operation of the individual Endeavorers

there. If the president of the society is a member of the executive committee *ex officio*, he will be expected to tell his society about the executive-committee plans and interest the society in them. If the society presidents are not members of the executive committee, the committee will see that in some way its plans are reported to every society. Some societies will be represented on the executive committee by officers and committee chairmen, but only a few. It will be necessary to arrange for regular visits to the other societies by representatives of the committee, bearing the message of the committee's desires and purposes. If the union is too large for this, then the secretary of the executive committee (the secretary of the union) will send to each society a printed or manifolded account of the committee meeting, and the plans in which the committee asks for the co-operation of the societies. Call for some written response, and follow up energetically the societies that do not make this response.

The State Executive Committee.—What has been said about the executive committee of the local union applies very fully to the larger unions of the county, district, and State. These will be made up of the union officers, and generally there will not be room for more. If the State union has denominational vice-presidents or representatives from different parts of the State, it will be a large and strong body. In some States it may be possible to include in the State executive committee the presidents of all the city, county, and district unions in the State, with a president's cabinet of the principal officers for quick action in emergencies.

Meetings of the State executive committee may well

be held in different portions of the State during the year, that all the members may find it convenient to attend at least some of the meetings, and that a number of cities may come into touch with the State leaders. The afternoon will be spent in planning for the State work privately, and the evening will be given up to a mass meeting with the members of the State executive committee as the speakers. Sometimes these meetings of the State executive committee may be held in connection with county or district conventions for which the members of the State committee will be the principal speakers, sandwiching in their committee meetings between the sessions.

Class Work on Chapter VIII

The Leader's Questions

Why is the executive committee " the heart of the union " ?

How large should the executive committee be ?

How often should the committee meet ?

Where should the executive committee meet ?

What should be the programme of an executive-committee meeting ?

What social features may add interest to the executive-committee meeting ?

What speaking may be obtained for the meeting of the executive committee ?

What special meetings of the executive committee may be held ?

How may the executive committee push the use of Christian Endeavor literature ?

What will the pastoral counsellor do in the executive committee meeting?

What will the executive committee do for the larger work of the union?

How will the executive committee aid the societies?

How will the State executive committee carry on its work?

Topic for a Talk or Essay

An Executive Committee That Executes.

Subject for a Class Debate

Resolved, that our union executive committee should be larger.

CHAPTER IX

THE UNION STRENGTHENING THE SOCIETIES

The Work of Union Lookout Committees.—The union lookout committee has functions precisely similar to those of the society lookout committee. Its business is to keep the societies of the union up to the highest level of efficiency, and also to add to the union as many new societies as possible. It does this by organizing new societies and by persuading those already organized of the advantages of membership in the union.

Not every union has a lookout committee, but all should have. Many a society has died because there was no outside organization to revive it when it fell into a decline. Christian Endeavor in many a locality has languished because there was no body of workers whose special duty it was to form new societies and stimulate those already existing.

This work is most educative. In the work of the church it is frequently necessary to revive languishing churches and Sunday schools. It is constantly necessary in every community to start new churches and Sunday schools. What better training for this important work than that of the union lookout committee? Every pastor should recognize the strategical value of this service for the kingdom of God quite apart from its undoubted value as a strength for Christian Endeavor.

The Organization of Union Lookout Committees.— The chairman of the union lookout committee should

be some one with a thorough knowledge of Christian
Endeavor and burning zeal for our society. His committee should be made up of persons likewise well
informed and zealous, though they may not all have
the chairman's ability as a leader. If the union is
small every society may be represented upon this committee, usually by the chairman of the society lookout
committee. If the union is large, then active Endeavorers from all sections of the city will be placed upon
the union lookout committee, and care should also be
taken to obtain upon that committee a good representation of all the denominations in the union. The committee will need a secretary, and it should hold regular
meetings at least once a month; oftener than this at
the beginning of the year.

Pastoral Counsellors.—Every union should have a
pastoral counsellor whose work will be so closely associated with that of the lookout committee that he may
well be made an *ex officio* member of it, besides sitting
with the union executive committee at all their important sessions and advising the president of the union
in all the union's important undertakings.

The pastoral counsellor is to represent the pastors of
the town or city in all the larger aspects of Christian
Endeavor. He will be chosen by the ministers' meeting
of the town, if there is one. Lacking that, he will be
chosen by the union itself, the different denominations
furnishing a representative in turn. Two years is a
good term of service.

The pastoral counsellor should be in hearty sympathy
with the society of Christian Endeavor. He should
also be a man held in honor by his brother ministers
and very influential among them. It is his work to

represent the union among the ministers and the ministers in all the affairs of the union. If the union executive, for instance, is in doubt whether the plan of a union Bible-study class would be approved by the pastors, they will turn for advice to the pastoral counsellor, who will give his opinion, usually consulting his brother ministers. If there is doubt regarding a proposed form of entertainment, it will be submitted to the pastoral counsellor. If some large enterprise is undertaken by the union, such as the establishment of regular work in a hospital or a country home for poor children, the pastoral counsellor will be consulted before any conclusive step is taken.

Also the pastoral counsellor will be exceedingly useful in the extension work of the union. When it is desired to establish a new society in a certain church, the pastoral counsellor will approach the pastor of that church and show him what a fine agency for good the society is. He will remove the misconceptions of Christian Endeavor that may exist in the minds of his brethren. He will defend Christian Endeavor in the denominational and ministerial gatherings and in the public press. He will be a tower of strength to the society.

Due honor will be paid to the pastoral counsellor. He will often be asked to take part in the mass meetings of the union. His name will be given a conspicuous position on the union stationery. Former pastoral counsellors will not be forgotten, but will often be brought into the union gatherings and shown that they are held in grateful memory.

It will be seen how useful a pastoral counsellor will be to the union lookout committee. While you will remember that he is a busy pastor, and will refrain from making unreasonable demands upon his time, yet

you will obtain his presence at the lookout-committee
meetings when you can, and you will take to him all
important committee matters. Above all, you will
seek to obtain his active advocacy of the society among
the pastors that have no society in their churches.

Openings for New Societies.—Probably there is not
a Christian Endeavor union anywhere, however well
the community is already organized for Christian Endeavor, but might be doubled if all the definite openings for new societies were filled. The most obvious
lack is of Junior societies. There might be a Junior
society in every church with a Young People's society.
As it is, less than half the Young People's societies are
matched by Junior societies. The union lookout committee does not need to hunt up the children. They
are there, and eager for the Junior society. What it
needs to do is to lay the blessed duty and privilege of
being a Junior superintendent upon some worker and
help him or her to organize a Junior society. Little
advantage is taken of the plan for conducting Junior
societies by Junior committees from the older Christian
Endeavor societies, thus dividing the work and responsibility of the superintendent. The proper advocacy
and use of this method would add many thousands to
the number of Junior societies now existing.

The same may be said of the Intermediate society.
This has a place in almost every church on account of
the desire of young people of Intermediate age to be
by themselves. It is of especial advantage in the
larger churches, where the graduates from the Junior
societies are lost in the Young People's societies, and
often fall from activity into a state of stagnation.

Few churches have maternal associations, and thousands of Mothers' Societies of Christian Endeavor should be formed, not only to act as aids of the Junior societies, but to give the mothers inspiration and direction in the rearing of children and the management of Christian homes.

The Senior Society of Christian Endeavor is for the reception of graduates from the Young People's society. Its prayer meeting is the regular church prayer meeting, to which it is a tower of strength. It is a great blessing to any pastor and a great aid to any church in which it is established.

Office societies of Christian Endeavor are of service in commercial establishments, bringing together the Christian employees and banding them together for the winning of their associates and for many other forms of helpfulness.

Societies formed among prisoners with the co-operation of the wardens and chaplains have proved of immense benefit to the inmates. Societies formed on sailing vessels, in street-car barns, in old ladies' homes, in hospitals, among the attendants in asylums of various kinds, in army posts, among the policemen and surfmen —all these have been greatly blessed by God. Intermediate societies in high schools have proved to be a stronger agency for the uplift of high-school pupils than any other ever tried.

All of these are forms of Christian Endeavor that are not fully developed, probably, in any community in the world. They offer a vast field for union lookout committees, a field full of inviting possibilities, easy and pleasant to work, and certain to yield rich returns.

It is also possible for the union lookout committee to change many a denominational young people's society into a Christian Endeavor society with the hearty approval of the pastor and the willing consent of the denominational authorities. This is because many denominations that have special denominational societies are entirely willing to enroll Christian Endeavor societies in their denominational organizations without change of name and without their dropping the Christian Endeavor interdenominational fellowship. If the union lookout committee explains this to the pastors and young people, backing up their statements with denominational literature, they can often extend the circle of Christian Endeavor and give to isolated denominational societies the tremendous advantages of our unions. Here the help of the pastoral counsellor will be most efficient.

Organizing New Societies.—When the lookout committee of the union has found an opening for a new society it may need to work quietly a long time before it has gained a foothold for Christian Endeavor. If the new society opening is in a church it will first, of course, learn the attitude of the pastor. If he favors it, the rest is easy. If he opposes, you must learn why he objects and must remove his objections. Here the pastoral counsellor will aid you, and you will be greatly assisted by obtaining answers to the pastor's objections from the State Christian Endeavor officers and the officers of the United Society of Christian Endeavor. Often printed matter can be obtained which will remove the pastor's misconception and answer his argument. It is, of course, useless to try to proceed till the pastor is heartily in favor of the step.

If the proposed society is to be organized elsewhere than in a church, there will usually be some head man to consult and win—the members of the firm if it is in a shop, the principal of the school if it is in a high school, the warden and chaplain if it is in a prison, the captain and chaplain if it is on board a vessel of the navy, etc. Patience and tact will win here, though you may need to work for months.

Then you need to work with the young people concerned (or the adults if the society is for adults). Experience shows that you will have no trouble here. The society carries its own appeal. Everywhere it is liked, once the conservatism or prejudice of the heads of institutions is broken down.

After obtaining by many conversations the gradual assent of the leaders among the young people (if it is to be a Young People's society) and their consent to join as charter members, you will call a meeting of all the young people of the church, leaving it with the young people already interested to give the invitation as widely as possible. To this meeting the union lookout committee will come in force. The chairman will speak enthusiastically of the value of Christian Endeavor, and various members of the committee will testify of the same, each speaking of the workings of the society in a different particular, so that the little speeches are cumulative.

Then you will have a word from as many of the young people present as will speak, saying that they propose to join the new society. Finally, you will call for a vote on the formation of the society, it being understood that all voting in the affirmative will join as active or associate members.

The next step is the adoption of a tentative constitution which has been drawn up in advance. This will be read, section by section, and adopted as read, with the understanding that it is subject to change as experience may direct. A nominating committee will be appointed and will bring in nominations for the first set of officers. These will be largely agreed upon in advance, as the launching of the new society depends so much for its success upon the ability and consecration of the first officers. The newly chosen president will then announce the first prayer meeting with its subject, and will call a meeting of the new executive committee for a certain night. The meeting will close with words by the pastor and with his closing prayer and benediction on the new organization.

With changes made necessary by the different circumstances, essentially the same process will be followed in the organization of a Christian Endeavor society of any type.

Organizing Campaigns.—It is well for the entire force of a Christian Endeavor union to be focused occasionally upon the work of organizing new societies. If a strong movement can be set on foot, some churches may be swept into the current that could not otherwise be touched. Besides, many Endeavorers will work with more zeal and industry if they know that many others are working with them.

Such a time is provided in each Christian Endeavor Week. The union lookout committee should look forward to this day and prepare for it through many preceding weeks. Lay plans for as many different kinds of societies as you can, and for new societies in as many churches as you can reach. Announce your plans and expectations as fast as they mature for the inspiration of the workers, but save for Christian Endeavor Week the completion of as many acts of organization as you can. What a glorious thing it would be if on Organization Day of that week a dozen new societies should be formed in your community! What golden fruit would spring from that day through all coming years!

Reviving Dead Societies.—It must not be forgotten that it counts just as much for the kingdom of God to revive a society that is dead as to form an altogether new society. Sometimes the society died because of the opposition of a pastor who did not understand Christian Endeavor. That pastor has gone to another church and the way is clear for the reviving of the society. Perhaps the society died because it got into the hands of old members who did not train young members to take their places. Now the old members have left the work, and a new society can be formed wholly of the young people. Perhaps it is a Junior society that was given up when the superintendent got married, and now you can start it again led by a Junior committee from the Young People's society.

This revival of a dead society may be attended with as much joy and exultation as the founding of a new society. Get the help of the former members. Incorporate them in the society, if they have not grown too old. At any rate, obtain their co-operation. Learn what mistakes were made in the conduct of the old society, and see that they are not repeated. Start the new society with the freshest and best methods upon the highway of a permanent success.

Surveying the Field.—The first work of the union lookout committee as it enters upon its task of bettering the societies is to learn in what particulars each society needs bettering. This it can do in two ways, by writing to the society and obtaining answers to a list of questions, and by visiting the society and getting the facts by observation and conversation. The first method is more rapid, but far less satisfactory. Probably it may wisely be used as an entering wedge, but it should always be followed up with personal visits as soon as feasible.

In asking for information from the societies the lookout committee will be guided by the information already available gathered by preceding committees. It will need to know the membership of each society, and the number of members of each class. It will need to know what committees each society has, and to get some idea what kind of work each committee is doing. It will need to know the average attendance at the prayer meetings, and the ways in which the members take part. It will need to know about gifts to missions and to the union work. It will inquire about the socials and the business meetings, and whether the executive committee meets regularly. And it will ask about the number of young people in the community and how well the society is filling its field.

Of course, with so much work to be done, the lookout committee must fix upon a few definite things to be attempted first, and its search for information will at first emphasize these points whatever other points may be included.

The societies may be divided among the members of the committee, one to each, and the committee will meet regularly once a week for a time to hear reports from the visitors and devise plans for helping the societies overcome the difficulties and correct the faults which these visits have discovered. If a member from each society is a part of the lookout committee of the union, this member will be made responsible for the carrying out in his own society of the committee's suggestions and for reporting on the matter to the committee from time to time.

Inter-society Visitation.—An excellent way of stimulating the societies is for the union lookout committee to arrange a scheme of inter-society visitation. Agreeing to this plan, each society in the union will receive at every prayer meeting for a time a delegate from some other society, and will send a delegate to some other society. The delegates will learn from the societies they visit, and will report to their home societies what they have learned. They will speak in the prayer meetings they visit and will tell about the work of their own society, giving points to the society visited. The plan will be continued till every society has received a visit from the representative of every other society in the union, unless the union is too large for that; at any rate, from every society in the same section of the city.

Furnishing Leaders.—At another time the union lookout committee may furnish to the societies prayer-meeting leaders from other societies. For this service those Endeavorers only will be chosen that are especially skilled in leading prayer meetings in original and helpful ways. Each leader that comes thus to a society will give its members new ideas and stimulate them to better work.

Lookout-Committee Conferences.—Early in the year the union lookout committee will hold a conference with the members of all the lookout committees of the societies in the union, or sectional conferences if the union is too large for a single conference. The union chairman may preside, and the different subjects discussed will be opened by Endeavorers from the different societies that have been especially successful along those lines. Many topics will be treated, such as how to enlarge a society, how to answer objections to the pledge, how to better the prayer meetings, how to keep members faithful to the pledge, how to make the associate members active, how to increase the spiritual value of the prayer meetings, and how to introduce new members to the society work. Leave ample time for a question-box or for the oral introduction of any perplexity that any one present may wish to bring up. Close with an acquaintance half-hour and light refreshments. Be sure to use the evening in part for interesting the members of the local lookout committees in the work of the union lookout committee, especially the forming of new societies.

Reports from the Societies.—When the lookout committee sets out to improve the societies in any special way, it will ask for regular and frequent reports from the societies along this line. This will be in addition to whatever reports the union secretary may be getting. For instance, if the union lookout committee is trying to get the societies to make more of the associate members, it will hear from the societies often regarding the status of those members, giving whatever plans have been found useful for leading them to become active and getting them to join the church. Of course the facts thus gathered may be desired by the union secretary, and if so should be handed over to him for incorporation in his statistics.

Membership Campaigns.—The union lookout committee may well stimulate the societies to enlarge their membership by instituting membership campaigns. To this end it will describe for the societies approved methods of work, such as " red and blue contests." It may offer some reward for the society that gains the largest number of new members by a certain day. The leaders of the different bands at work in these local efforts may hold a conference on methods, over which the union chairman will preside. On the conclusion of the campaign the results will be reported at a union meeting, and some of the experiences of the workers will be related.

Efficiency Campaigns.—Similar united efforts for improving the efficiency of the societies may be organized by the union lookout committee. Use for this purpose the general model of efficiency set forth in the efficiency chart of the United Society. Ask the societies to make as much progress as they can in percentage within a certain time. Hold a meeting of the chairmen of the local lookout committees for the fixing of the present percentages of the societies, the union chairman passing on doubtful points. With these per cents as bases the contest will start, the society that gains the largest number of per cents being declared the winner. This contest also, with its results and experiences, will furnish material for an interesting union meeting.

Expert Classes.—Every society should have a class in the United Society's text-book, " Expert Endeavor," once a year, and the union lookout committee should first have a class for the training of leaders of these society classes. An experienced Endeavorer will lead the training class. Several chapters will be discussed at each sitting, and a thorough examination will be held at the close. Those that pass will receive the degree of Christian Endeavor Expert, and will be allowed to wear the Expert pin. Many thousands have pursued this study with great pleasure and profit. The societies will take it up readily, and the union lookout committee can do nothing better for the work than to develop these classes in " Expert Endeavor." The study introduces the best methods for each officer and committee and line of work, as well as dealing in the history and principles of Christian Endeavor.

Lookout Work in the Union Meetings.—Whenever the lookout committee of the union has a point regarding the improvement of the societies or the growth of the union that it especially wishes to make, it should take advantage of the union mass meetings and get in a bright talk on the subject. The betterment of the prayer meetings, better singing, more prayers in the meetings, personal evangelism, fidelity to the pledge— such subjects as these make the very best themes for the union meetings, and may well occupy the very best speakers. Whoever prepares the union programmes will be glad to carry out occasional suggestions from the union lookout committee along this line.

Then, too, the lookout committee may wish to interest certain societies in the union, and to that end may bring them into the union meetings for the furnishing of certain features—taking part in an open meeting, or furnishing a series of one-minute talks, or getting up a chorus to sing.

A Union Pledge.—The union lookout committee may well make use of the great power of the pledge in its work of arousing and maintaining interest in the union on the part of the societies. Propose to the members of the societies some such pledge as the following : " Believing in the fellowship of the churches and the co-operation of Christians, and desiring to unite with the Endeavorers of other churches in work for Christ's kingdom, I promise loyalty to the Christian Endeavor union of _____, by customary attendance and hearty support."

That is a reasonable pledge, as all Endeavorers will admit. Present it at a meeting of the union executive committee, and win their enthusiastic approval. Have it presented to each society by an earnest speaker, who will tell how much the union work means to Christian Endeavor and to the cause of Christ. Distribute the pledge on slips of paper with pencils, and call for signatures on the spot. Refer to the union pledge often in the union meetings, and make it as strong a feature of union work as the society pledge is of society work. You will find the gains to be immediate and large.

Co-operation with Other Union Committees.—The lookout committee will not duplicate the work of other union committees, but will merely co-operate with those that approach its own line of work. For example, if there is a union music committee it will help the societies in their music, and the lookout committee will not touch this particular field. So with the union missionary committee, social committee, finance committee, and the like. On the other hand, these are all matters in which the societies should be stimulated by

the union lookout committee, if there are no union
committees doing the work.

County, District, and State Lookout Committees.—
Every county and district union should have a lookout
committee, which will be in close connection with the
union lookout committees, and will work through
them, but will also aid the societies in the rural
regions not reached by the city unions. It is in this
work that the county or district lookout committee can
be especially useful. New societies need to be established in these outlying regions. There is many a
country schoolhouse where a society might be formed
that would prove to be the greatest blessing to the
community, doing much of the work of a church, starting and maintaining a Sunday school, perhaps in time
establishing a new church there.

The executive committee of the State union usually
takes on itself the functions of a State lookout committee ; but if it does not, then a State lookout committee should be formed. The work of this committee
would be to co-ordinate the work of the district and
county and city union committees, and keep them up
to the full measure of their tasks. What the other
lookout committees do for societies, in forming them
and stimulating them to do their best, the State lookout committee will do for unions, establishing new
ones where they are needed and putting the best methods into all of them. There is great need of such a
committee in every State union, for usually the State
secretary or the field secretary is left to do this heavy
work alone, together with much besides that is far too
burdensome for one man.

Class Work on Chapter IX

The Leader's Questions

What is the work of the union lookout committee?

How is the committee organized?

What is the work of the pastoral counsellor?

What kinds of new societies may be formed?

How may a new society be organized?

How may a dead society be revived?

What surveys of the field should the lookout committee make?

How may the union lookout committee aid the societies directly?

What conference should the lookout committee hold?

How is a membership campaign conducted?

How is an efficiency campaign conducted?

How is an expert class conducted?

How can the lookout committee aid the union meetings?

What is the union pledge?

What is the work of the lookout committee in the larger unions?

Topic for a Talk or Essay

The Committee That Looks Out and In.

Subject for a Class Debate

Resolved, that our union needs an efficiency campaign.

CHAPTER X

UNION WORK FOR THE CHURCHES

A Union Church–Work Committee.—Since Christian Endeavor has for its motto " For Christ and the Church," our unions should be doing some work directly for the churches of their community and the denominations to which they belong, and to further such work it is well to appoint in every union a church-work committee. This committee should be headed by some active and versatile church worker, and should have such workers for its members, taking them from a wide range geographically and denominationally. This chapter describes only a small part of the work this committee may do, for that work depends largely upon local circumstances and will develop constantly with the interest and zeal of the workers.

Denominational Committees.—One of the first pieces of work that the union church-work committee may do is the establishing of denominational committees in the societies. These committees will be in close touch with the denominational boards, especially the boards of home and foreign missions. They will keep track of what these boards are asking from the churches and the young people's societies, and they will see that the Endeavorers carry out these wishes so far as their own societies are concerned, and in their churches also so far as they can exert influence. This committee in each society will attend to the local circulation of denominational papers, and will see that items of denominational news are reported in the Christian Endeavor prayer meetings from time to time. They will also keep well informed regarding the needs of the local church, so far as the Endeavorers can help to meet them, and will be a church-work committee as well as a denominational committee. Conferences of these denominational committees will be held once or twice a year under the leadership of the union church-work committee, and here plans will be discussed and adopted for the helping of the churches on the largest scale possible to the Endeavorers.

A Church Workers' Conference.—It is always astonishing to learn how many of our Endeavorers are already officers of the church or members of church committees. Once a year the church-work committee of the union will hold a conference of these Christian Endeavor church officers, for the sake of discussing their duties and stimulating them to better service. At this conference have representatives of the different officers give little papers or talks each on his own work, which will then be freely discussed. Some church treasurer will talk about the raising of church money; some deacon will discuss the work of deacons and how it may be better done; a church chorister will discuss church music, and so on. The union committee will have a few veteran church officers present with their advice.

In the Ministers' Meetings.—The union has a representative of the ministers in its pastoral counsellor; it would be well if the ministers could have a representative of the union in their ministers' meetings, and the president of the union would be the most suitable representative. Of course, the pastoral counsellor is there; but some young man in the closest possible touch with the Endeavorers would be helpful to the ministers many times, and would gain much for the union from this inside view of the hopes and desires and opinions of the pastors. This representation cannot well be asked by the union, but the offer of it should be promptly accepted if it comes from the ministers.

A Religious Census.—Occasionally in every rapidly growing community a religious census should be made, and the forces of the Christian Endeavor union, representing usually all denominations, would be ideal for making this census. Under the guidance of the pastoral counsellor the entire city or town will be mapped out, blanks will be furnished and carefully explained, the Endeavorers will be drilled in the work expected of them and the streets will be divided among them. Each house will be visited, the church relations and preferences will be learned, and the possibilities of new Sunday-school pupils and new members of the Christian Endeavor societies will be discovered. Frequent reports will be made as the work progresses, and the whole will be accurately summarized for the ministers' meeting and given in detail to the pastors concerned.

Church Invitations.—The church-work committee of the union may get the churches to unite in an invitation, to be signed by all the pastors, which will state where religious services are held each Sunday and where prayer meetings are held during the week, the time of each service being stated and a cordial general invitation extended. All this will be printed attractively as a folder, perhaps with pictures of the churches and the pastors. The church-work committee will obtain the help of the societies, which will take the work in turn, and copies of this circular will be placed in the mail-box of each hotel guest, and laid at the table for each boarding-house inmate in the city.

Church Bulletin Boards.—Permanent bulletin boards advertising the services of the different churches should be placed in the railroad stations of every town, hung up in the post-office, and put in the shop-windows where the merchants are willing. This is work that the union church-work committee can do with the co-operation of the pastors. Each pastor will be glad to supply a cut of his church. Some printer will print the cards at a low rate. The union will do the framing at its own charges and will put up the bulletins. These advertisements of religious work will turn many toward the house of God, and influence many a life for the right.

The "Help-Our-Church" Movement.—The union church-work committee may establish "help-our-church" movements in the societies. The purpose of this is to set the young people to considering what they can do to help their own churches. Fix a definite time for this. Doing it all together will be sure to stimulate many societies that otherwise would not undertake any work for their own churches; and when once they are started along this line they are likely to keep up the work. Each society is to find out from its pastor what it can do for the good of the church, and is to do it within the time set. Then, at the end of the time hold a union meeting and listen to the glowing reports of what has been accomplished. Some will have planted flowering bushes in the church-yards. Some will have bought new hymn-books for the pews. Some will have painted the church. Some will have bought new chandeliers. Some will have started a church paper. Some will have made a canvass for the increase of church contributions. Some will have persuaded a number to join the church. The work done will vary widely, but it will all be delightful and profitable work, meaning much for the future as well as the present.

Go-to-Church Sunday.—A union church-work committee will be able to organize " go-to-church Sunday " and make it a great success, as it has already been in many localities. It will advertise the idea widely in the secular papers and church papers, by posters and circulars, and in all the meetings of the church. The pastor will preach special sermons, special music will be provided and special decorations, and the Christian Endeavor society and the Sunday school will have special features. All this will be worked up by the Endeavorers under the direction of the pastor and with the co-operation of other church workers. The result is always a greatly increased attendance on that Sunday, and some permanent additions to the congregations.

A Church Prayer-Meeting Campaign.—At another time the church-work committee will emphasize the clause of our pledge regarding church services, and especially the midweek prayer meeting of the church.

Each society will be asked to divide itself into four bands, one for every week of the month. Members of each band will not only attend the church prayer meeting that week—this is always expected—but will take part. Arrange with the pastor to call upon them to take part immediately after his opening talk. Their participation will be brief and pointed, and, while not taking much time, will give the meeting a brisk start that will be welcome to the older members present. Moreover, it will be the beginning of regular participation on the part of many Endeavorers.

Life-Work Recruits.—No larger work can be done for the churches and the denominations than the winning of new candidates for the ministry and for missionary service. This the Christian Endeavor society seeks to do through its work for the obtaining of Life-Work Recruits. The union church-work committee will see that this subject is brought up often in the meetings of the union and in the prayer meetings of the societies. Whenever the prayer-meeting topic is appropriate, which is often, the societies will be reminded of this great cause, and the leaders of the meetings will be asked to emphasize it. Personal work may be done in co-operation with the pastors, seeking to influence toward a life-work decision those whom the pastors point out as most fit for the work of a minister or a missionary.

Tithing Crusades.—The Tenth Legion, our Christian Endeavor enrollment of tithe-payers, will be pushed in every union. Some unions have Tenth Legion superintendents, and all unions should have, even the smallest unions; for the problem which the Tenth Legion would solve, if universally adopted, is one that particularly affects the churches of small towns. The Tenth Legion superintendent will see to the appointment of Tenth Legion superintendents or committees in all the societies. These will approach every member with the plan of tithe-paying and the arguments for it, and will try to get him to try it at least for a month. Few that try it ever go back to the old haphazard method of giving.

Song for the Churches.—The union music committee may set the music committees of the societies to doing much for their churches, particularly by holding song services before the church doors to attract passers-by into the evening services. Choruses may be formed to help out the evening meetings and church prayer meetings, and in many other ways the singing Endeavorers can aid the church.

Aiding the Sunday Schools.—If the Sunday schools do not seem able to support separate teachers' meetings, the union church-work committee may plan and conduct a union Sunday-school teachers' meeting that will be a great blessing. The chapter on Bible study details the plans for union Bible-study courses, which also will greatly aid the Sunday schools. The union church-work committee may bring about the formation in the Sunday schools of Christian Endeavor classes which each week will study the lesson for the next Sunday, so as to be ready to furnish substitute teachers. So many of the Endeavorers are teachers and officers in the Sunday schools that a union conference of them may well be arranged for the discussion of improved Sunday-school methods.

An Interchurch Mothers' Meeting.—Where the churches do not seem disposed to establish separate mothers' associations, the union church-work committee may form a successful interchurch maternal association, bringing together the mothers of the community once a month to listen to wise and helpful talks on home life and the care of children, following these with free and full discussions and ending with light refreshments and a social good time. These mothers' associations will be very helpful to the Junior work as well as to the mothers.

See Other Chapters.—Many other chapters in this book contain hints for the work that unions may do for the helping of the churches and denominations. These undertakings are not under the care of the union church-work committee but of other union committees, such as the press committee, the evangelistic committee, and the music committee. If these other committees do not take up this work, the union church-work committee may suggest it to them; or, if the others do not care to undertake it, they may do the work themselves.

Class Work on Chapter X

The Leader's Questions

What is the work of a church-work committee?

What work may denominational committees do?

What conference will the union church-work committee conduct?

What may the union do in a ministers' meeting?

How is a religious census made?

How can the union church-work committee increase church attendance?

What is the "Help-Our-Church Movement"?

How can the union aid "Go-to-Church" Sunday?

How is a church prayer-meeting campaign carried on?

How can the union promote the enrollment of Life-Work Recruits?

How can the union promote Christian beneficence?

What can the union do to improve church singing?

How can the union aid the Sunday schools?

What is an interchurch mothers' meeting?

Topic for a Talk or Essay
A Christian Endeavor Church.

Subject for a Class Debate
Resolved, that the primary loyalty of the Christian Endeavor society is to the church work and not to the society work.

CHAPTER XI

UNION WORK FOR MISSIONS

The Union Missionary Committee.—Every Christian Endeavor union should have a missionary committee for the promotion of missionary work in the societies, and for the accomplishment of missionary work that the societies can do in co-operation but cannot do singly. Missions are the great field of Christian endeavor, and therefore they should never be forgotten by any organization of Christian Endeavorers.

The union missionary committee will be made up, if the union is not too large, of the chairmen of all the missionary committees of the constituent societies of the union. If the union is too large for this, then select for the union committee the most active and successful local missionary chairmen from all sections of the city, being careful to represent each section well. Pains must be taken also to represent each denomination fairly in this union missionary committee; and sometimes the union in a large city will form denominational union committees, each made up of the local missionary chairmen of the societies of one denomination. The chairmen of these various denominational committees, with possibly a few others, are then brought together as the union missionary committee.

The head of the union missionary committee will be called its chairman, or he may be designated as the missionary superintendent of the union. He (or, of

111

course, it may be a young woman) must be first of all a missionary enthusiast ; and second, he must be a good executive, able to conceive plans and get others to help him carry them out. Particularly he must realize that he has not succeeded till he has communicated his own missionary zeal to all the societies of the union. This is a great work, and he will look upon the chance to do it as a blessed opportunity.

Missionary Committee Conferences.—Perhaps the first work of a union missionary committee should be to hold a conference of all the chairmen of the society missionary committees. If the union is small and the chairmen of these committees are members of the union missionary committee, then hold a conference of all the members of the local missionary committees.

The chairman of the union missionary committee will preside at this conference and will lead the discussions. Have a definite plan for the conference. There is nothing better than a series of questions on topics such as " How can we interest the Endeavorers in missionary books ? How can we promote missionary giving ? How can we better the missionary meetings ? Plans for missionary socials. Setting the Endeavorers to praying for missions. Getting into touch with the denominational missionary boards."

The list of topics will be printed clearly on a blackboard or a large sheet of paper, or duplicated so that every one present can have a copy. Well-informed Endeavorers may be invited beforehand to open the discussion of the different topics, but only with a minute of informal talk, not with set speeches. Fill the evening with brisk question and answer, the giving and receiving of experiences and suggestions.

This conference should be held very early in the society year, before any missionary meetings have been held in the societies; and therefore an important feature of the evening may well be the discussion of plans for the coming missionary meetings. Appoint one person for each of these meetings, whose duty it will be to come with a budget of plans for that meeting. These plans will be presented to the conference and discussed, and others will add to them. Possibly another conference may be held for these special plans, and only the leaders of the year's missionary meetings invited—a conference of missionary prayer-meeting leaders.

Generally one missionary committee conference of this sort will be enough for the year; but it should be held early, so as to start the work in the societies with enthusiasm and with full information.

A Missionary Speakers' Bureau.—A large union may organize a speakers' bureau especially for missionary speakers, to be furnished to churches and Christian Endeavor societies in need of such assistance. This bureau will consist of one or more persons who are in close touch with the mission boards and who are likely to know when good speakers on missionary themes are in town or are readily obtainable. If a returned missionary is in the vicinity, or if some one has just come back from a journey in missionary lands, or if some missionary-board secretary is passing through the town, the speakers' bureau will arrange to have as many societies as possible enjoy the opportunity for fresh, first-hand missionary information and inspiration. Contact with a live missionary is one of the most valuable experiences that can come to a Christian Endeavor society, so that the work of this speakers' bureau is very important. If it is not established as a separate institution in your union, at least its work should be done by the union missionary committee.

A Missionary Information Bureau.—Some unions have extended the speakers' bureau into a general information bureau on the subject of missions. The Endeavorers constituting this bureau will be well informed regarding missionary literature. They will be able to give inquirers just the help they need in working up talks on any missionary subject. They will know about the different mission boards and their publications. They will be posted regarding all kinds of helps for the study of missions. If they do not know a fact themselves they will know where to find it, which is almost as well. The bureau will be readily reached by telephone, and its members will be there one evening a week ready to talk to inquirers.

A Union Missionary Library.—The missionary information bureau, or, lacking this organization, the union missionary committee itself, may well gather a union missionary library which will be at the disposal of all the societies for the preparation of their missionary meetings and for missionary socials or other missionary entertainments. The library will be bought by union funds, and will be enlarged by gifts from the societies and from interested individuals. It will contain as many missionary books as possible, especially missionary biographies, accounts of missionary lands, and a full set of the mission-study text-books. The library will be rich in a well-arranged collection of the many valuable pamphlets and leaflets published by the various boards, and in missionary scrapbooks or envelopes, full of classified clippings on missions.

A Union Missionary Exhibit.—This same missionary information bureau may add to its duties the gathering of a missionary exhibit, or such an exhibit may be brought together by the union missionary committee. It will be found very useful for the illustration of all kinds of missionary gatherings, and may well be utilized in the Sunday schools as well as the Christian Endeavor societies. The exhibit will come to contain, by gift and purchase, a great variety of objects illustrating life in missionary lands; especially native costumes, so useful in missionary exercises. Maps of mission fields will be added, and a valuable collection of stereopticon slides bearing on missions, with a union magic lantern for lending wherever it will be of use. Such an exhibit will be drawn upon constantly, and, if presided over by a wide-awake curator, will be a most helpful factor in the union activities.

Circulating Missionary Meetings.—It will be the business of the union missionary committee to know when especially bright and original missionary meetings are given in the various societies, or especially interesting features are presented in any missionary meeting. These may then be repeated in other societies as the missionary committee of the union may arrange; and every repetition will serve to promote fresh missionary zeal and ingenuity in the visited society, while at the same time the society thus " encored " will feel it an honor and will be moved to new exertions. In the same way particularly successful leaders of missionary meetings may be " passed on " around the union.

Union Missionary Meetings.—Such features as the foregoing will also be used to brighten the union missionary mass meetings which will be held from time to time with general audiences. The cause of missions is so important that it may well occupy one union mass meeting every year. Inspiring speakers, stirring choruses, bright and pointed talks by representatives of the different societies, fervent prayers, graphic illustrations —all will serve to render this meeting the most popular the union conducts.

The union missionary mass meeting is held at a time that will not interfere with the regular church services. The societies unite in paying for the speaker, unless the expenses can be borne by the union treasury. Give an opportunity for questions from the floor after the speaker is through. If you cannot obtain a speaker of undoubted interest, you can make up a delightful programme from the best features presented in the society missionary meetings of recent months. The meeting is likely to be successful in proportion as it is well advertised in the societies, in the church pulpits, and in the church and secular papers, as well as by posters.

Union Decision Meetings.—One of the great purposes of Christian Endeavor is to raise up a host of recruits for the ministry and for missionary service. One of the union mass meetings occasionally may well be devoted to this aim. Get a speaker who can present powerfully the needs and opportunities of mission fields, and can appeal convincingly to the conscience for decisions for the missionary life. Do not call for open announcements of decision, but in a period of silence call upon all to consider prayerfully their own responsibilities in this connection. Urge those that feel impelled to dedicate themselves to definite and life-long missionary work to consult their pastors, and take steps to learn how many in the union have made this great decision. Every union may well form a Volunteer Band of prospective missionaries.

Neighborhood Missionary Meetings.—The interdenominational fellowship of Christian Endeavor may show itself occasionally in neighborhood missionary meetings, the societies of several near-by churches of different denominations getting together for a joint meeting in which each society will tell something about the most interesting missionary work of its own denomination. Thus the horizons of the societies will be widened and their interest in missions deepened. Such neighborhood meetings are easily prepared, since each society will contribute some of the most successful features of the missionary meetings it has already held.

Union Missionary Socials.—Socials give a fine opportunity for the dissemination of missionary information and the cultivation of missionary interest. A union missionary social will give the idea of such socials to many societies, and one may be held by the union missionary committee once a year, either in connection with a union meeting or independently. Different societies through their missionary committees may be made responsible for different features of the social, as for supplying booths representing foreign countries, giving bright exercises, furnishing mission songs, arranging a display of curios, or leading in some native game. The social may be based upon some mission land such as China or India, and of course you will choose some country that is most in the popular eye.

United Prayers for Missions.—A very impressive union missionary meeting may be arranged at some time of severe missionary crisis, as when there are massacres on some mission field, or the natives are suffering under famine, flood, or pestilence, or when some great war is in progress. Then the societies may be called together to think of their distressed brothers and sisters, and especially to pray for them. Some earnest speakers may be heard, but most of the time should be spent in faithful prayer by the Endeavorers. It would be very appropriate to hold such a meeting at a time when missionary contributions have fallen off and the boards are in great straits for sorely needed money.

Missionary Reading Contests.—The union missionary committee may greatly stimulate missionary reading in the societies by offering some reward to all those that will do a certain amount of missionary reading of a quality to be fixed by the committee; or the reward may be offered to the Endeavorer who reads the largest number of missionary books within a certain time, regard being had also to the value of the books read. The committee will offer to lend interesting books and 'missionary magazines, and will send to each society a list of the best missionary books available in the public library and the various Sunday-school libraries. A model list of books may be furnished to the Endeavorers entering the contest. The reward may be copies of missionary books. They should be presented at a public meeting of the union, when special emphasis will be laid upon missionary reading.

A Union Missionary Entertainment.—Christian Endeavor unions have special facilities for presenting missionary entertainments—cantatas, pageants, and similar performances which popularize missions. Different parts will be assigned to the various societies so as to interest as many as possible in the entertainment. Each society will be expected to sell a certain number of tickets, and the proceeds may be used for the missionary work of the union.

Christian Endeavor on Mission Fields.—Among the missionary interests of every Christian Endeavor union some place should certainly be found for the missionary work of the United Society of Christian Endeavor, which makes so many grants to mission fields at home and abroad for the support and increase of Christian Endeavor work there. Missionaries of all denominations testify that our society is of the greatest help to them, especially in the training of the converts. The grants of money made by the United Society for the spread of Christian Endeavor in the parts of the world that are not as yet able to maintain their own national Christian Endeavor organizations are of prime advantage to the missionaries of all denominations, and contributions for this object may appropriately come from all our Christian Endeavor unions. A missionary pageant or other entertainment will serve to raise the money. Some large unions interest themselves in the support of Christian Endeavor in special mission countries, and even pay the salaries of the Christian Endeavor travelling secretaries there. If more unions would do this a heavy burden would be lifted from the officers of the United Society.

The Union Promoting Missionary Giving.—The missionary fundamentals are money, men, and prayers, as

is often said. Our unions have a work to do in connection with all three, and not the least in regard to
giving, since as young people are taught to give out of
their small incomes so will they give when their incomes
rise into thousands of dollars.

Every union may well have a Tenth Legion superintendent, whose sole business for the union is to promote membership in this important branch of Christian
Endeavor. If there is such an officer he should be a
member *ex officio* of the union missionary committee.
If there is no such officer, some member of the committee will be detailed for the work.

Urge the appointment of Tenth Legion committees
in the societies, or at least of special committees for the
promotion of giving. Urge the societies to increase
the number of members of the Tenth Legion among
them, and to that end choose some appropriate topic
from the uniform list and ask that the societies remember the Tenth Legion on that evening, having its members explain it and make an earnest effort to get more
tithe-payers, using the "ballots" which the United
Society sells for the purpose of promoting decisions.
Keep a record of the number of Tenth Legioners in
the union, and report how it stands from time to time.
A banner may be offered to the society containing the
largest proportionate number of tithe-payers. That
the missionary committee may have a basis for its
financial appeals, arrange with the union secretary to
collect with his other information full statistics about
the missionary gifts of each society—the amounts, and
the causes to which each has contributed.

Uniting to Support Missionaries.—Of course it is not
feasible for an interdenominational union to support a

denominational missionary, but the societies of one denomination in the union may be brought together and encouraged to assume under the direction of their mission board the entire or partial support of some missionary or native worker at home or abroad. These denominational groups within the union may vie with one another in this glorious work, each striving for the greatest zeal and efficiency.

Union Mission-Study Classes.—One of the most useful things a union missionary committee can do is to organize a union mission-study class for the training of leaders for society mission-study classes. At least one such class should be formed every year, preferably two, one in home missions and one in foreign missions.

Active advertising and personal work will bring together from the societies the possible leaders of local mission-study classes. The teacher will be the best you can find—zealous for missions and able to impart his zeal to others; well informed regarding the subject he is to teach, and skillful not only in the art of teaching but in the yet more difficult art of training teachers.

One of the many admirable mission-study text-books will be used, and you will naturally choose the one for the current year, or one bearing on some country or field particularly interesting at the time. The eight lessons will be taken in eight weeks, or, perhaps better, in four. You will take ample time for each recitation —two hours is not too long. You will not neglect the important questions and answers. You will make full use of maps and other illustrative devices. You will seek to give the members of the class an adequate equipment for teaching the same book in their own societies.

Call for frequent talks from the members of the class. Let each take his turn as often as possible in teaching the class some section of the chapter under discussion. Close the study with strict examinations. Above all, follow up the work and see that in every society represented in the class, if possible, a mission-study class is taught by some member of the class within the next few weeks. No better way of diffusing missionary zest and information has ever been found than this, and no agency for the work is better than our Christian Endeavor unions.

Helping City Missions.—Numbers of city rescue missions make use of the Christian Endeavor societies to help them in their work. The young people go often to the meetings of the mission, sing and testify and make as strong an appeal with their fresh, strong, and innocent faces as with their pointed arguments and earnest entreaties. The good the Endeavorers get from this contact with actual soul-saving work far more than balances the good they may give. Such a service may well be organized by the union missionary committee for all rescue missions that desire it. The societies thus interested in the mission will want to aid in its support and will interest their churches in the work.

Where there is no rescue mission the Christian Endeavor union, under the direction of the pastors, may start a mission and maintain it, hiring a superintendent and aiding him in every way. This is a glorious work which will do more to make a union strong and efficient than perhaps any other work it could undertake. It includes the maintaining of recreation rooms for men and women, girls and boys. It includes Sunday-

school work for the children.   It includes helpful visiting among the poor.   It includes outdoor playgrounds
for the poor children.   It includes classes in useful oc-
cupations.   It includes much civic reform work that
will be found to be necessary.   Indeed, there is no end
to the blessed outgrowths of such an undertaking.

**County, District, and State Missionary Superin-
tendents.**—Much of the foregoing applies without
change to the missionary superintendents in county
and State unions and to the meetings and other operations of those unions.   The State missionary superintendent, however, is to work directly with the missionary committees of city, county, and district unions, and
not with the individual societies except as these are not
connected with unions.   The State missionary superintendent will find that his first duty is to establish as
many missionary committees as possible in the unions
that have not yet appointed them and start these committees in their duties.

The State missionary superintendent will gather up
from all sources the fullest possible statistics of the
Christian Endeavor missionary work of the State.   He
will note the best missionary work done in the different
unions and will send accounts of it to the other unions,
acting as a clearing house of good methods.   He will
learn of good missionary speakers visiting the State,
and will arrange for as many unions as possible to hear
them before they leave the State.   He may plan and
carry out a missionary rally at the State convention,
and a conference of the missionary workers present
from all over the State.   He will gather a State missionary exhibit, getting material from the boards and
from the local societies.   He will send bulletins of good

missionary ideas to the union missionary committees. In short, he will do for the various union missionary committees about what those committees do for the societies under their care.

Class Work on Chapter XI

The Leader's Questions

How is the union missionary committee made up ?

How will the committee conduct missionary conferences ?

How will it manage a speakers' bureau ?

How will it carry on an information bureau ?

What will the union missionary library be and do ?

What will be the contents and the work of a union missionary exhibit ?

Describe circulating missionary meetings.

How will the union missionary meetings be conducted ?

Describe union decision meetings.

What will neighborhood missionary meetings accomplish ?

How will union missionary socials be carried on ?

What is the value of united prayer for missions ?

What contests may the committee conduct ?

How may the committee conduct missionary entertainments ?

What is the relation of the union to Christian Endeavor on mission fields ?

How may the union promote missionary giving ?

How may the union support missionaries ?

How manage a union mission-study class ?

How can the union aid city missions ?

What is the work of missionary superintendents in the
larger unions ?

Topic for a Talk or Essay

Christian Endeavor for the World.

Subject for a Class Debate

Resolved, that our union should start some missionary
enterprise of its own.

CHAPTER XII

UNION WORK FOR SOUL-SAVING

Why Union Evangelistic Work?—Every Christian Endeavor society worthy of the name will be an evangelistic agency, because evangelism is the Christian endeavor that is nearest to the heart of Christ. But the evangelistic impulse is generally given to a society from without, if it comes at all, and it should be given by the Christian Endeavor union. Moreover, it is far easier for each society to do evangelistic work if all the other societies are doing it at the same time. The evangelistic spirit is contagious. More than that, wise evangelism requires training, and the leaders in this work in all the societies can be trained by union effort. Still further, there are large evangelistic operations that are too great for any one society, but can be conducted by the joint effort of all the societies in a union. For these reasons every Christian Endeavor union should place evangelism among its aims and among its definite operations.

The Evangelistic Committee.—The committee of the union placed in charge of evangelism will have for its chairman a very wise young man, a devout Christian, a person of great common sense, loved and respected by all. He must not be a faddist. He will have the confidence and esteem of the pastors, and will be able to obtain their co-operation. His associates upon the committee will be Endeavorers of his own stamp, and will represent every section of the city, possibly every society in the union. Each society representative may be the chairman of the evangelistic committee in his own society, and thus the plans of the central committee will be carried out in each society.

A Class in Personal Evangelism.—The United Society's text-book in evangelism, " 2 Tim. 2 : 15," by Rev. H. W. Pope, is finely fitted for use in a union class in personal evangelism. Every member of the union evangelistic committee will join the class, of course, and every member of the society evangelistic committees, together with all other Endeavorers that can be persuaded to come. The leader will be some one of experience in soul-winning, so that he can illustrate out of his own experience the many practical points of the text-book. He must be some one approved by the pastoral counsellor of the union.

Take a chapter an evening, and have the members of the class read it at home, think it over, and come prepared to discuss it thoughtfully. The leader of the class will have many pointed questions to be answered, and will give ample opportunity for the asking of questions by the Endeavorers. The great purpose of this class is to train leaders in this work, who will go out into their own societies to lead just such classes, and thus to stimulate the Endeavorers to undertake personal evangelistic work for themselves.

Personal Workers' Bands.—One great task of the union evangelistic committee is to form personal workers' bands in the societies. These bands are made up of the Endeavorers, however many or few, who will agree to make an earnest and continuous effort for the salvation of at least one soul, and to meet regularly with the others of the band to pray for this work and consult one another about it, each reporting his own experiences (probably without naming the person or persons for whom he is working). If a member of the personal workers' band fails, or seems to fail, in his attempt to win some soul for Christ, he will get the help of some one else of the band, and then if necessary of another. What one cannot do because of personal limitations another may do with the greatest ease.

These personal workers' bands may meet once a fortnight, and their organization will continue for years if the Endeavorers are faithful. You will invite to join the band only those who you are sure are deeply interested in this work and will be faithful in it. You will add to the band from time to time, as you discover others of the evangelistic temper. No one is to join the band merely to interest him in evangelistic work, but he will be interested by other means.

And it is very necessary that the work of the band shall be secret. It will make no report. Its membership will not be known. Even its existence will be kept secret, as far as is feasible without introducing the element of mystery. You will fail with the friends you are trying to bring to Christ if they feel that they are the subjects of organized effort and not of personal interest.

An Evangelistic-Committee Conference.—When the union evangelistic committee has got these society evangelistic committees to working, it will be in order to hold a conference for instructing their members and stimulating them to better service. An evangelistic pastor may well give the opening talk, relating some of his own experiences in personal evangelism and afterwards joining in the discussion. It will be well for the leader of the conference to have a set of suggestive topics or questions to start the discussion ; but if the societies have been doing active work for soul-winning, they will have enough questions to fill up many hours.

Outdoor Evangelism.—The Christian Endeavor type of prayer meeting gives splendid training for effective outdoor evangelistic meetings. The Endeavorers can get permission for such a meeting, if permission is needed. They can draw the crowd with singing some bright songs. They can bring in cornets, fifes, drums, and other instruments, including a baby organ. They can have many brief prayers and short ringing testimonies, such as they give in their Christian Endeavor prayer meetings. The leader can close with an earnest appeal for the Christian life. Such meetings as these, persisted in week after week, cannot fail to do a vast amount of good. They will win attention by their modesty, simplicity, and earnestness. Men will listen to young folks when they might not listen to other men.

Shop Meetings.—Meetings may be arranged for shops during the noon hour, when the workers, having finished their lunches, are ready for any diversion. The meetings will be of the same nature as the outdoor meetings, but will be of a more familiar character because of the quiet of the shop compared with the street-corner. You will have a chance here to make acquaintances, if you come week after week, and you can meet and talk with those that wish to know more about the Christian life.

Tent Meetings.—Christian Endeavorers have been very successful in tent work, and are the back-bone of most of those enterprises. The work is usually done during the summer, and sometimes the tent is peripatetic through the rural districts, though usually it is stationary in the heart of a city. Most frequently an evangelist is employed, the Endeavorers being his faithful assistants. They furnish the singing, they hand out invitations on the streets, they act as ushers, they give brief testimonies and offer brief prayers, they visit from house to house, inviting people to the meetings, and in many other ways they aid the evangelist. If no evangelist is employed, nevertheless the union might well conduct a series of tent meetings with only Endeavorers to speak.

In Rescue Missions.—Those glorious institutions, the city rescue missions, are always glad of the help of Christian Endeavorers. The union takes charge of the matter, and assigns now one society and now another to send a delegation. This delegation sings heartily, sometimes furnishing special music, and its members give brief, earnest testimonies—both singing and testimonies being strictly under the direction of the superintendent of the mission. The Endeavorers will also be helpful in obtaining for the mission openings in the churches for the presentation of its cause and for the gifts of the church members. All churches should have a share in rescue-mission work, and the Christian Endeavorers that take a personal part in the work will get from it far more than they can give.

Evangelism in the Societies.—The ordinary work of a Christian Endeavor society calls for much real evangelism, especially in the operations of the lookout committee. Every time a candidate comes before the society for associate or active membership, the questions of allegiance to Christ, confession of Christ before others, and the joining of the church will be sure to come up. As the Endeavorers deal faithfully with these matters, they will have many a chance to plant the seeds of truth in receptive minds. They can turn many from associate membership into active membership and into the church. Young people seldom realize their power over other young people, but are too cowardly about speaking for Christ. The union evangelistic committee can do much to promote evangelistic action in the lookout committees of the societies, and through them among the other Endeavorers.

Class Work on Chapter XII

The Leader's Questions

Why shall we do union evangelistic work?

Of whom should the union evangelistic committee consist?

How carry on a class in personal evangelism?

How conduct personal workers' bands?

How conduct an evangelistic conference?

What outdoor evangelism should the union carry on?

How conduct shop meetings? tent meetings?

How can the union aid rescue missions?

How can we promote evangelism in the societies?

Topic for a Talk or Essay

Saved—to Save.

Subject for a Class Debate

Resolved, that young people can best be won to Christ by other young people.

CHAPTER XIII

UNION BIBLE STUDY

Why Union Bible Study?—There are many reasons why our Christian Endeavor unions should conduct Bible-study classes perhaps as often as once a year. In the first place, there is the argument of experience, since many unions have done this work, to the great profit of their members and to the advantage of the churches. We have never heard of an unfavorable criticism or of dissatisfaction with the results.

In the second place, it is probably not too much to say that most of the Sunday-school teachers in our Christian Endeavor churches come out of the Christian Endeavor societies. For their own honor, therefore, as well as for the sake of the work at large, the societies should see that the workers they send into the Sunday school are as well trained as possible. Of course if the Sunday schools of any locality are carrying on an adequate teacher-training course, the Endeavorers will not duplicate it; but the Sunday schools seldom do this, or if they do it, they seldom continue year after year. Teachers' meetings in the Sunday schools are few, and in most instances the Christian Endeavor union can undertake the union Bible-study class in the confidence that it is doing a unique and greatly-needed work that will not be undertaken by any other organization.

Another reason for the union Bible-study class arises from the difficulty of obtaining well-equipped and in-

spiring teachers for such classes. When you find one,
you will be wise to make the most of him and give
him the largest audience possible.

Moreover, there is great value in numbers. Bring
together in one class scores of Bible-lovers from many
societies and denominations, and it is like gathering
live coals in a heap ; a big fire is sure to result. New
thoughts are flashed from mind to mind, and the
contagion of Bible zeal rapidly spreads.

And finally, not to mention other reasons that may
be given, we must remember that the very promises
of our pledge, calling upon us to pray and read the
Bible daily, constitute ours a Bible society. Many
thousands of us also have taken the special pledge of
the Quiet Hour. It behooves us to vitalize the pledge
by learning all that we can about the Bible, getting
the broadest views of it and discovering how to obtain
from its sacred pages all the wisdom and power stored
up there for us. These union Bible-study classes will
greatly enrich the private devotions of our members
and will widen out into all our Christian Endeavor
prayer meetings.

Pastoral Advice and Oversight.—The only danger
attending this work is that some teacher may be
chosen that will not be approved by the pastors of the
churches involved. Very properly the pastors would
rather there should be no union Bible-study class than
one taught by a man who would use the opportunity
for the inculcation of theories about the Bible which
are simply masked infidelity, or a man of no imagination or adequate scholarship whose stock in trade is
bald literalism, or a man who would devote most of
his time to teaching some religious fad. It is of prime

importance that the teacher should be a reverent, force-ful, clear-headed Bible scholar, who will command the respect of all the pastors and the affection of all the young people. The pastors can probably guide in the discovery of such a man. If the Endeavorers have a man in view, they should obtain the hearty assent of their pastors before engaging him or even approaching him in the matter.

If your union has, as all unions should have, a pas-toral counsellor appointed by the pastors themselves to serve as their representative in the union counsels, then his advice and consent will be all you need. If you have no such officer, you will need to go to the ministers' association ; or, if there is no such body, then to the individual pastors. You may grudge the time and pains necessary for this, but time and pains are necessary in starting any undertaking. Remember that every such instance of respect shown to your pastors will strengthen their regard for the union and their confidence in Christian Endeavor.

After the teacher of the class is chosen, still continue to make full use of the pastors. Give them a cordial invitation to all sessions of the class. Always have one of them present (a different one each time), on special invitation, to open the class session with prayer. Ask them to announce each meeting of the class from the pulpit and in the church prayer meeting as well as in the church calendars. Do everything you can to make them feel that this is their work, in which the young people look to them for guidance and for gen-uine leadership.

Who Should Teach the Class?—You will seek, to teach the union class, some one with a youthful heart, with a deep love for the Bible, with sufficient Bible scholarship, and with the teacher's skill. Avoid absolutely the teacher who will be destructive rather than constructive. Avoid the talkative teacher, who will lecture rather than question and seek to parade his own wisdom rather than make his pupils wise. Avoid the conceited man, the opinionated man, the trifling man. You will probably not be able to find the ideal Bible teacher, for he is not often found ; get the best approximation you can discover, and remember that other years are coming in which you may find in your Bible teachers the qualities lacking in this year's teacher, though he in turn will have some good qualities which they will lack.

The Cost of the Course.—You may be able to obtain the very best teacher without a cent of cost, but it may be necessary to get some one from a distance at considerable cost, if only for his travelling expenses and entertainment. If the latter is the case, then, before you enter into an agreement with your teacher, make sure that you can pay him.

Announce the proposed class in a circular to the societies or by personal visits to the different societies. State what the expenses will be, and call for subscriptions or memberships in the class. Each person joining the class will pay a certain sum for the privilege, perhaps fifty cents. Non-transferable tickets will be issued, admitting each member to the class. It will be clearly understood that this admission fee is in addition to the cost of whatever book is used in the class.

Some unions will be strong enough financially to engage the teacher and pay him out of the union treasury. This will sometimes be the best course; but, generally speaking, the Endeavorers will value more what they have each paid to obtain, and will be more faithful in their attendance if each has purchased a ticket of admission.

The Length of the Course.—It is far better to have a short course of perhaps eight lessons than a longer course which may drag at the end. Attempt no more than you can carry through with a triumphant swing. And eight lessons, occupying four weeks, two lessons a week, are better than eight lessons occupying eight weeks. Of course in this matter you must be governed largely by the convenience and experience of the teacher of the class.

The Subject of the Course.—Here you will be guided by the teacher you have obtained, who may offer you your choice of several courses which he is ready to give. If you are able to select your own course, we advise you to avoid an ambitious subject covering much ground and choose a rather more restricted theme which can be pursued with a fair degree of thoroughness, so that the Endeavorers will feel the satisfaction of having carried the subject to completion.

Your subject may be one book of the Bible. It may be some phase of Bible literature, such as the parables. You may take a rapid survey of the prophets. You may study the orations of the Bible. You may take a fascinating course in Bible geography. You may study some of the contrasted characters of the Bible. You may get an outline view of Bible history, or of the life of Christ or of Paul. You may choose some subject especially helpful in connection with the current Sunday-school lessons. You may select a topic of current interest, such as the Bible teachings on war and peace.

Books for the Class.—Whatever the subject, each member of the class will be required to bring a copy of the Bible, and it will be well to insist upon the Revised Version, either the English or the American Revision.

In addition, each member of the class must purchase a copy of any text-book used. If a book of the Bible is chosen, the text-book will be some brief commentary upon that book. The teacher will choose the text-book and the union will probably be able to get a discount from the booksellers or publishers.

Then each pupil will be expected to have a note-book and to take full notes of all the teacher gives the class and of the class discussions. These notes should always be reviewed before the next lesson.

Conducting the Class.—Every teacher will have his own methods, but for a successful class certain elements of teaching are essential. At each lesson some home work should be assigned to be done in preparation for the next lesson —some Bible reading and some bits of research and original thinking. In the class a large use should be made of questions to provoke discussion and prompt to thought. Now and then the brighter pupils will be asked to prepare brief essays on themes connected with the study, and read them to the class. The map will be used wherever it would add to the interest and understanding. All analyses should be written clearly upon the blackboard and copied carefully. Some teachers make too much of analyses, which renders their instruction dry and forbidding. Others make too little of such written helps, thus rendering their instruction vague and leaving little in the memory. There is a wise mean between the two extremes.

Above all, the teacher should not give so much that he really gives nothing at all. Crowding the lesson with thoughts and facts, tersely presented, merely serves to discourage all but the keenest minds. The teacher must remember that few, if any, in his audience .are familiar with the subject, and that a little well presented and really carried away is far better than a large amount of thought and learning poured out upon his pupils only to roll off unreceived.

Concluding the Course.—After the final lesson of the course, the class may meet some evening for a fellowship gathering to express their appreciation of their teacher. You may have light refreshments, and the evening may be enlivened with music and song. A few appropriate talks may be given, carefully prepared beforehand and bearing on Bible study in general, or the course you have just followed in particular. A little organization may be formed for the purpose of maintaining the class and adding to its numbers when next you meet in the succeeding year.

At the next union meeting held after the close of the course the work of the class will be reported to the union by one of the members, and you may well spend fifteen minutes also in hearing brief testimonies regarding it from all that will give them.

Class Work on Chapter XIII

The Leader's Questions

Why should our unions engage in Bible study ?

Why should this Bible study have the advice and oversight of the pastors ?

What kind of teacher should be found for the class ?

How will the cost of the course be met ?

How long should the course be ?

What subjects may be used ?

What books will be needed ?

How will the class be conducted ?

How will the course be concluded ?

Topic for a Talk or Essay

Partnership in Bible Study.

Subject for a Class Debate

Resolved, that union Bible study is needed to supple-
ment the Bible study that is now carried on.

CHAPTER XIV

UNION CIVIC AND TEMPERANCE WORK

Why a Union Temperance and Citizenship Committee?—Most work for the betterment of a town or city requires for effectiveness the massing of forces, and so this kind of work is especially suited to Christian Endeavor unions. It is begun in the local societies, but they must combine for any large result.

When there is talk about appointing this committee, some will be sure to object against "mixing religion and politics." But why should not religion be mixed with politics? Every one agrees that politics needs the purification and uplift that religion would give. Is any one afraid that religion will be worsted in the contest or fouled by the fight? Wherever there is wrong to be made right, there religion should go; and many wrongs are to be made right in and through politics.

Of course the church and the Christian Endeavor societies ought not to mingle in mere struggles for office where personal ambition is the only motive and the spoils of office are the only issue; but wherever moral questions are at issue and the welfare of man is at stake there Christians are needed, and there they should take their stand as Christians and band themselves together as Christians to bring about the better condition of affairs that Christ Himself desires.

Christians are of all parties, and are conscientious in their party allegiance. True Christian citizenship work will not disturb these party allegiances in most cases. It will bring together the honorable men of all parties, to fight for the basal principles of good government that should underlie all parties. There is and can be no partisanship in such a struggle. It is an interparty work, as Christian Endeavor is interdenominational and international and interracial. It can and should be entered upon in the spirit of the Reformer of Galilee.

The Make-up of the Committee.—Work on the union citizenship and temperance committee calls for considerable maturity. It would be well to confine membership to voters, and you will place upon the committee the most experienced young men of all the societies. Every society should have its own citizenship and temperance committee, and the union committee may well be made up of the chairmen of these local committees. If the union is too large for this, then take leading citizenship workers from the societies in different sections of the city. The chairman will be some one well informed regarding civic and political conditions, wholly consecrated and courageous, an effective speaker and a practical worker for civic betterment. The work itself, if you once start it, will rapidly develop good leaders.

Citizenship and Temperance Conferences.—Perhaps the first work of the union citizenship and temperance committee will be to get similar committees appointed in all the societies. Some voter should be the chairman, and the rest of the committee should be made up of wide-awake young men and women deeply interested in the affairs of town or city. These committees will plan for the enrichment of all prayer meetings that have civic or temperance topics, and will combine in the union temperance and civic work. A conference of these committees should be held as early as possible to form plans for real work for civic betterment. Some of the suggestions given below may be laid before this conference, or some other plan that may be suggested by local needs.

Under Advice.—The civic work of the union, perhaps more than any other kind of work, is full of pitfalls for the inexperienced. It should not for this reason be neglected, but it should be undertaken with the advice and under the supervision of the wisest adults you can interest in your activities. Here is one place where the pastoral counsellor of the union will come in. Of course all plans that involve wide action and considerable publicity will be passed upon by the union executive committee, after consultation with men of mature judgment and especially with the pastoral counsellor.

Civic Study Classes.—A very useful plan, to which no one can take exception, is the formation of union classes for the study of civic conditions and of the great reforms, especially the temperance reform. For such classes excellent text-books are available, particularly the temperance text-book published by the United Society of Christian Endeavor. The leader, who should be most carefully chosen, will be some one of conspicuously pure motives, of thorough knowledge, and of courageous character. He should be some one who will inspire the young people with a zeal for the highest type of citizenship, and who will lead them along ways of practical civic efficiency.

A short course of perhaps eight weeks will be enough each year. Take up some concrete subject of study, such as the temperance reform, the public-school system, the prisons, or the question of public franchises. It is better to learn a few things thoroughly than many things superficially. The teacher of the class will bring in experts to talk to the young people and answer their questions, especially the public officials in charge of the matter under consideration. You will introduce little essays and speeches, you will have debates, and you will make use of many articles in periodicals and all other books, besides the chosen text-book. Try to lead up to some practical outcome, some immediate use of the Endeavorers' new knowledge. Make this union class a training-school of leaders, each of whom will go to work to conduct a similar class in his own society.

Civic Studies.—Sometimes it will be possible to follow up a class in civics with a series of careful studies of different sections of a city or of different phases of city life. For this purpose those that are willing to undertake the work will be banded together under competent leaders. They may learn the location of the saloons in the city with reference to the churches, the schools, the residences, and the stores, and may draw such conclusions as they can with regard to the influence of the saloons on these different neighborhoods. They may study the city's drinking fountains, or parks, or system of caring for the poor. They may study the slum district in its many aspects. The main conclusions of these studies may be presented to the union in a series of addresses.

Civic Themes in Union Meetings.—The union citizenship and temperance committee will be influential in bringing important civic subjects to the attention of the Endeavorers through the union mass meetings. These subjects will be suggested by current events, and will have close relation to current reforms. They should be treated by men and women of ability and experience whose words will have weight with thinking people and whose names will do credit to Christian Endeavor. Avoid extremists and fanatics and " cranks," however eloquent and persuasive they may be. In presenting a subject to young people whose minds are not yet trained to balance arguments and criticise coolly, it is especially necessary to take dispassionate views and give fairly both sides of every question.

Christian Endeavor Debating Clubs.—The old-fashioned debating club did much for our fathers and grandfathers; it will do as much for the young people of to-day wherever it is introduced, and Christian Endeavor unions are in a position to introduce it. The union debating club will draw from all the societies their most thoughtful young people, those most deeply interested in public questions. It may well meet once a month throughout the year. Every evening may have a formal debate with four speakers, two on a side; and also, to close the evening, the informal discussion of the same or a different subject in which every member of the club may join so as to get practice in general debating. An especially good debate may be repeated before the union.

Christian Endeavor Civic Leagues.—Christian Endeavor Civic Leagues are organizations formed for the study of public questions and for concerted civic action.

The most appropriate study to begin with is that of the town or city government under which you are living. Spend an evening, for instance, with the public-school system. Ask some member of the school board or the school superintendent to come and explain it to you and answer your questions. On another evening study the town taxes under the lead of the town treasurer, or the election system, or the courts, or the care of the poor, or the streets, and so on. Each meeting will have for its principal speaker some one whose business or office renders him thoroughly familiar with the subject under discussion; and each meeting, after his explanation, will close with a series of questions addressed to him by the Endeavorers.

The civic action of such a league will depend upon the community opportunities and needs. Some possible lines of work are indicated below. One thing you might do which would be full of helpfulness to young voters would be to learn all you can about the candidates for election upon whom they are soon to vote. Get some well-informed man to tell you about them, and at the next meeting balance his views by a similar talk from a man of another party. Ask questions about the different candidates, particularly regarding their attitude toward the great reforms. If you cannot find out in any other way, you can address polite letters of inquiry to the candidates themselves. This is not partisan political action, but is simply gathering the information which is gathered for the voters by the good-citizenship organization, if one exists, made up of men of all parties. The information you receive is not to be printed or published in any way; it is solely for the private instruction of the young voters in your societies.

Village Improvement Societies.—If your community has no village improvement society or a similar organization, the citizenship and temperance committee of the union may well start one. The object of such an organization is to unite all progressive citizens in working for the betterment of the town. You may aim at better sidewalks, cleaner streets, more shade trees, the abolition of fences. You may put up town bulletin boards. You may install public receptacles for rubbish. You may start a movement for the beautifying of yards. You may go on to more ambitious projects, such as a larger schoolhouse or a town hall.

Other Civic Enterprises.—If you have no public library, the union citizenship committee may inaugurate a movement to establish one. A recreation room may be connected with it. If the town has no park or common, such a place for public recreation should be provided. If the children have no good playground easily accessible to all, the Endeavorers will be doing a work most appropriate to them if they set on foot a movement for the forming of such a playground. Many towns have no public drinking fountains, and the Endeavorers have established them as a temperance measure. Sometimes these fountains are supplied with ice-water in the summer.

Petitions and Pledges.—The circulation among the Endeavorers of a good citizen's pledge may mean much for civic betterment in the future. This pledge may read: " In obedience to our Lord Jesus Christ, the Supreme Ruler, I promise to strive to be the kind of citizen He would approve, to try to do my full civic duty promptly and faithfully, and especially to seek to learn the characters of all candidates for public office that I may vote as Christ would have me vote."

The circulation of petitions in favor of good measures is work for Christian Endeavorers, and thus they may bring to bear upon unwilling politicians an influence that they cannot resist. The ready writers among the Endeavorers should be encouraged to write to public men brief, manly letters urging them to vote and work for any definite reform measure the writer has at heart, or praising them for any courageous action on behalf of the right. The papers may be used also for both these purposes; and of the two, the praise is more likely to be effective for the right than the blame.

Union Work for Temperance.—A very effective piece of temperance work is the placarding of the town with temperance posters. There are many of these now (they are for sale by the United Society), and they present in a very forcible way the strongest arguments for the temperance reform. Many of them are diagrams, and speak to the eye as well as to the mind. These posters can be placed in the shop-windows, on church bulletin boards, on the trees of private property near the streets, and in any other place where they will be read by large numbers. Each one of them will be a powerful temperance lecture.

Some unions have gone farther and have set up temperance signboards, which are large enough to be seen hundreds of feet away, and which state temperance facts and arguments briefly and convincingly. Sometimes these are electric signboards and preach their temperance sermons through the night.

Temperance maps may be prepared showing the number of saloons in the place, each marked by a black circle. The churches will be marked by gold circles and the schools by blue circles. These maps also will be put in public places where many will see them and be moved by their silent appeal.

As election approaches a temperance parade may be organized, the young people turning out with a brass band and with many pointed banners and transparencies bearing temperance mottoes and briefly-put temperance facts.

Whenever the question of no license is up, the union may combine heartily with other forces in a no-license campaign, or may carry on one by itself if no other agencies are at work. Mass meetings will be held addressed by the best temperance speakers available, placards will be used everywhere, a parade will be held, outdoor meetings will appeal to the workers, and temperance tracts appropriate to the situation will be sent through the mails or distributed at the doors of the houses. Get the leading citizens to sign an appeal for the driving out of the saloon—the most influential citizens, whether they are church people or not. Make a face-to-face canvass for votes, and try to reach personally all you can. If you fail, then try again next time, having learned the lessons of your failure. If you succeed, then keep your eyes open and see that the law is enforced.

Class Work on Chapter XIV

The Leader's Questions

Why should the union engage in civic and temperance work?

How should the union citizenship and temperance committee be made up?

What advice should be sought in this work?
How will union civic study classes be conducted?
What city study can be carried on?
How will the citizenship committee aid the union meetings?
What work can Christian Endeavor debating clubs do?
Describe a Christian Endeavor Civic League.
What is the work of a village improvement society?
What other civic work may a union do?
What is a civic pledge?
What work may the union do for temperance?

Topic for a Talk or Essay

The Christian Endeavor Citizen.

Subject for a Class Debate

Resolved, that civic conditions in our community call for action by our Christian Endeavor union.

CHAPTER XV

THE UNION SOCIALS

Why Union Social Work ?—Our Christian Endeavor unions do not often have social committees, probably because the union officers think that social work belongs to the societies alone. As a matter of fact, there are many kinds of social activity that societies can carry on only in co-operation, and these constitute the legitimate sphere of the union social committee. The entire union needs to have a warm social atmosphere, just as much as a society. Quite often, even where the societies are cordial and the members know each other well, the union meetings are stiff and the members of the different societies seem afraid of one another. In such a union it is impossible to carry out large enterprises with any fervor. The members do not know one another well enough to work together. It is the business of the union social committee to promote the acquaintance of societies just as the society social committees promote the acquaintance of members. This work, like all other union work, looks forward to the time when the young folks will be doing a similar work for the churches of a community and of a denomination.

The Union Social Committee.—At the head of this committee will be placed some one with a gift for the social management of large bodies of people, and this gift is a rare one. It is, however, cultivated by work on the social committees, and the best social committee chairman developed in the societies should be placed in charge of the union social committee. The members of the committee may well be the chairmen of the social committees of the societies, or, if the union is too large to have all of them on the union committee, then include social-committee chairmen from all sections of the city and from all denominations.

Social-Committee Conferences.—Very early in its term of office the union social committee should hold a conference of all the social committees of the union. The opening talk of the conference may well set before the Endeavorers the highest ideal of their work, that they are to be "social to save." Then will follow an interchange of experiences, each telling about the best social they have conducted or describing some little feature of a social. Questions will also be asked regarding the perplexities that develop in the course of the work. The chairman of the union committee will make sure in advance that three or four bright new socials will be described by workers from different societies; members of the union social committee will probably furnish these accounts. Make the conference of practical value to the workers, so that they will go away eager to put into practice the fresh ideas they have obtained.

Improving the Social Atmosphere.—The fundamental purpose of the union social committee should be to raise the social standards of the community, if they need elevation. In many communities the young people have no social ideas above card-playing, theatre-going, and dancing. These fill their lives with such frivolity that genuine religious work among them is almost impossible. When this is the case, the union social committee has before it a task of great and fundamental importance, and its members will need all the consecrated ability they possess to bring the young people to see the fun in better amusements. This object of the committee must not, of course, be proclaimed from the housetops, but be held as a quiet, steady purpose in their minds.

Worth-While Amusements.—The union social committee will work through the local social committees wherever it can, introducing the best type of games and sports to take the place of those of little or no value; but there is much that it can do on a large scale. For example, it can form a union Christian Endeavor chess club to arouse interest in that king of intellectual games. A union checker club or crokinole club would also turn the minds away from games of chance. A union tennis club is a possibility, owning its own courts and carrying on a fascinating series of tournaments in which all the societies will be interested. Similarly, a union baseball or football club may be organized, or a series of baseball or football games arranged between different societies. It may even be possible to get up a Christian Endeavor golf club with a club house and grounds, if you live in the country where land is readily available. Union bicycle clubs have often been formed by Endeavorers, and have combined noble religious work with their pleasure,—riding out to country schoolhouses and holding meetings there, forming new societies in outlying regions, and making their wheels ministers of light to a wide area. A union gymnasium is an easy possibility if the town has no gymnasium, and will prove very popular among the girls as well as the boys. It should be managed by some one of experience, who believes in gymnastics for the development of the whole body and not merely for the performance of competitive feats. From this to union field days is but a step, the different societies and Endeavorers training for field-day sports like running, jumping, vaulting, throwing, swimming, and climbing. If this is made an annual event, each year will see an increase of interest in it.

Union Excursions.—The members of the union are brought close together by pleasant excursions. These may be by boat, electric car, or steam car, and they will go to any beautiful and interesting spot in the vicinity. Some unions make these annual affairs, and get from them money profit as well as pleasure. An outdoor song service with a few brief, earnest talks and prayers will add much to the excursion. Union picnics are equally enjoyable, though they entail more labor. Union hikes will be popular with the boys at least, and with some of the girls. They should be managed by good walkers, and none but fairly good walkers should take part. They will set out for definite goals; and if the goal is an interesting natural object or some historical building or scene, so much the better. Less strenuous walks, in which any one may take part, even if of little pedestrian ability, are those devoted to some object of natural history. Bird walks are delightful. For this purpose a number of bird enthusiasts will lead, each taking a manageable group. The object will be to visit the bird haunts of the neighborhood and become acquainted with as many bird forms and bird songs as possible. Botanical walks and geological walks will be similarly conducted, and if the leaders know their business they will be great successes. Stargazing evenings, in which the union members are taught the principal constellations and allowed to look at the stars and planets through a telescope or even a lot of field glasses, will be much enjoyed provided the leader knows his subject well and knows how to interest others in it.   Microscope clubs, if formed throughout a union, will also lead to delightful walks.   This side of union social life has never been developed as it might be in any community.   It would do much to elevate the social standards of the young people.

Eating Together.—Light refreshments or even full meals may be arranged by the union social committee to the great advantage of the union.   Officers' suppers may be provided by the committee, and thus the executive committee brought together soon after business hours for a long evening of profitable discussion of union affairs.   At another time the social committee may bring together for a supper all the society presidents in the union, a presidents' conference following.   Committee dinners of various kinds may be held, the chairmen of different kinds of committees throughout the union being brought together under the joint auspices of the union social committee and the union committee that will conduct the conference after the meal.   Lawn fêtes may be made very beautiful and very pleasant, and may contribute to the union treasury if necessary.   A union supper may be an annual affair.   Some church will throw open its kitchen and dining-room and the union social committee will co-operate with the local society.   Some " get together " game will entertain the Endeavorers as they arrive, and after the supper the union annual business meeting may be held, followed by bright little speeches which leading workers are invited to prepare. Sometimes, if the union is small, light refreshments may be served in the church vestry after the mass meeting, with the sure result of doubling the attendance!

The Social Committee in the Mass Meeting.—The social committee has work to do in the union mass meetings, even if refreshments are not served. Sometimes the mass meeting may end with a social. Often it ends with a reception to the speaker of the evening, and of course the union social committee acts as master and mistress of ceremonies. Always the social committee will properly have charge of the important matter of ushering, receiving the various societies at the door and showing them seats, giving them hymn-books, and doing all that can be done to make them feel at home. Some little special attention may be paid the delegates. A flower may be pinned upon the buttonhole of each, or a badge for the evening made of paper cut in some design appropriate to the evening's theme. If it is a patriotic rally, a tiny flag may be pinned upon each. Sometimes each will be given a slip of paper on which he will be asked to write a question for a question-box on Christian Endeavor problems, or a definition of " Christian Endeavor " or of " Consecration," or an answer to some question bearing on the evening's subject, the best of these to be read later in the meeting. The social committee that exercises its wits devising means of making the Endeavorers feel at home will do much toward popularizing the union meetings.

Union Socials.—In addition to all these other possible activities of the union social committee there are, of course, the union socials, which occupy evenings by themselves quite apart from the mass meetings or committee meetings. The object of these socials is to act as models for the society socials, to put new ideas into vogue, and train social workers for the societies. They should be held as often as is necessary to accomplish these results. For instance, if you want to introduce the fine plan of missionary socials, have a sample one in the union; or musical socials, or State socials, or book socials, or socials of any other type that may be out of the ordinary.

Neighborhood Socials.—It is an excellent plan for the churches of a city neighborhood belonging to different denominations to hold neighborhood Christian Endeavor socials. These neighborhood socials introduce the young people of different churches to one another and bring about a better neighborhood feeling. The union social committee will divide the city into these " neighborhoods," and will appoint the churches that will entertain the neighborhoods first. Denominational socials are planned in the same way, except that they take in all the churches of one denomination in the city. The union church-work committee will plan them if there is one; but if not, then the union social committee.

Convention Reunions.—The delegates that went together to a national convention, especially if it was at considerable distance, got well acquainted on the way and would enjoy reunions, at least for a few years after the happy event. Usually after two or three of these annual reunions the delegates become too scattered for a reunion. The evening is spent in eating

supper together and then in "reminiscing" about the
convention. Sometimes it is best to hold a "reunion
evening" of the delegates to all recent national Christian Endeavor Conventions. The delegates to the different conventions meet socially in different rooms,
and then come together in a central room for bright
talks. Of course a supper may be the initial feature
of the evening.

Round Robins.—A pleasant feature of union work
may be a "round robin," which is a circular letter
started by some one and passed from one to another
in a prescribed order, each reading all that has gone
before and adding his own message. After the round
robin has gone the rounds and come back to the starter,
he takes off what he wrote at first, adds another message, and sends it again on its round, each person on
receiving it taking off his first letter and adding another. So it may continue indefinitely. Workers of
the same kind may best support such a round robin;
for example, all the society presidents in a union, or all
the corresponding secretaries. The letters will be
about the work which the writers have in common.
The social committee of the union will set these round
robins on foot in whatever circles the committee thinks
will be benefited by them.

Pageants.—Pageants are so popular, and deservedly
so, that they may well be utilized in our Christian Endeavor work. A single society could hardly undertake
one; but a union could do it well, under the auspices
of the union social committee. The pageant might
represent Christian Endeavor in its interesting history
and in all lands, or it might be based on local, State,

or national history. It should be given in the open air, with proper surroundings, costumes, and music. The Endeavorers will enjoy it, and it may be made to add considerable to the union treasury.

A Recreation Room.—Most communities have no common recreation room such as the Y. M. C. A.'s of cities afford, and the Christian Endeavor union may easily get such a room, pay the rent, fit it up with games, and the members of the union take turns in presiding over the room, keeping order and helping the young folks to have a good time. The room will be especially for the use of boys who have no good homes to go to, and it may be made a genuine means of Christian fellowship and helpfulness. The union social committee is the proper division of the union forces to set this plan on foot and carry it out.

Union Introduction Committees.—The union may have an introduction committee (see Chapter XX), or the social committee may undertake its functions. The important work of this committee is to keep in communication with other unions and with the societies in places that have no unions, and thus learn when any Endeavorer removes to the town in which the introduction committee works. The new-comer will bring a letter of introduction from his old society. The introduction committee, receiving this letter, or, without the letter, learning of the presence of the stranger Endeavorer, will at once put him into touch with a society of his denomination, introduce him to the Endeavorers there, see that he is made a member of that society, and do all they can to make him feel at home in the town. The union introduction com-

mittees of a State should be advertised in the State
Christian Endeavor organ, or in the State papers, from
time to time. Every union at least should have a list
of the introduction committees in all other towns of
the State.

Class Work on Chapter XV

The Leader's Questions

Why should a union do social work?

How should the union social committee be made up?

How will the committee conduct conferences?

What will the committee do to improve the social
atmosphere of the town?

How will union excursions be conducted?

What use will the committee make of eating together?

How will the social committee aid the union mass
meetings?

How will union socials be conducted?

How are neighborhood socials carried on?

What are the advantages of convention reunions?

How are round robins managed?

How can the pageant idea be utilized?

How can a recreation room be conducted?

What is the work of the union introduction committee?

Topic for a Talk or Essay

" Social—to Save."

Subject for a Class Debate

Resolved, that our union should establish a recreation
room.

CHAPTER XVI

THE UNION MUSIC

Why Union Work for Music ?—Why should not the union let the church that entertains the union meeting furnish the music and let that answer? Why should the union go into the work of providing music and arousing a strong musical interest among the societies? Because if the union does not do it, in the majority of cases no other agency will do it. Few churches have any musical interest that extends to the young people and seeks to develop their musical ability for Christ. Comparatively few Christian Endeavor societies have music committees; and those that have, do little work besides seeing that the meetings are provided with pianists. And even if in some societies this fine musical interest existed, it would not exist in all of them, and some agency is needed to pass it along. And even if all the societies were interested in developing their musical powers, there would still remain much that the societies could do all together for good music that they could not do separately. There is therefore ample justification for a union's "going into" music and making a strong feature of it.

The Union Music Committee.—While the chairman of the union music committee should be some one with a real love for music and some musical training, he need not be a song leader, for he can get some one to do that work for him. But it is essential that he be a good executive, able to arouse the interest of the young people and hold it fixed upon music. His committee may well consist of the chairmen of the society music committees, and one of the first bits of work his committee should do is to see that every society in the union has a good, strong music committee, even if some of the members must be taken from other committees or work on two committees at once. It is well to add to the union committee as advisory member some good choir leader or other singer or musician who is interested in developing the musical interest of the community. The advice of such a person will be worth much in the choice of music and in the general management of your musical enterprise, even if he has no time to work with the union in more continued ways.

A Music-Committee Conference.—To this conference all the members of music committees in the union will be invited. The leader of the conference will be the chairman of the union music committee. Some of the best workers will be prepared to make brief speeches when called upon to open the most important of the discussions. On the blackboard or on a large sheet of paper print a list of questions about Christian Endeavor music, such as: " What are the advantages of society choirs? What gains come from special music in the meetings? Why is it well to have music leaders in the societies? How can we make fuller use of our hymn-books? How can our societies help the church and the community with their singing? How can we get our members to sing better? How can we put the devotional element into our singing? " Other questions will be added as the local needs suggest. Distribute copies of some song-book, and introduce illustrations of good songs, properly sung, throughout the conference as the musical director of the union suggests. Leave ample room under each topic for general discussion. Send the Endeavorers away with their heads full of practical musical plans for carrying out in their societies.

For Better Society Music.—In ways even more direct than the music-committee conference, the union music committee will seek to further the cause of good music in the societies. It may be feasible for the union to obtain the services of some expert song-leader who will go about among the societies, spending an evening with each. The regular prayer meeting will be given up on this occasion almost entirely to singing under this expert guidance, and many hints for musical improvement will be obtained. At some other time the union music committee may organize a quartette, which will go about among the societies giving special music at their meetings in order to stimulate them to do the like with home talent. Again, the union committee may get a good musician to go among the societies organizing society orchestras wherever possible— and it will be possible in a surprisingly large number of societies. Let every meeting of the union music committee bring out at least one good plan for the music of the societies, which the chairmen of the society music committees can take back with them and put into practice.

Neighborhood " Sings."—Often it will stimulate the musical interests of the societies if the young people of several societies—those whose churches are near together—meet in some vestry or private house for a good evening of song. Use the society song-books; and you may use several in the course of the evening, the Endeavorers looking over together. Each society will choose its favorite songs from its own book. It will be a good drill at sight singing. Of course you will need to have an expert and enthusiastic leader. The union music committee will appoint these neighborhood groups throughout the city, and some members of the union committee will always be present to make the " sing " a success.

A Union Singing-School.—The union music committee will do much for the musical zeal and ability of the societies if once in a while it organizes a union singing-school. The instructor should be of the best, and a small fee should be charged to pay him and to make the Endeavorers value their privilege. The school should meet once or twice a week for several months, and the best of music should be practised. The teacher should have in mind the singing in the society prayer meeting, and should often give hints regarding it. The school may end with a concert, the proceeds to go to the union or to the instructor, as may be arranged.

Union Hymn-books.—It is a good plan for a union to own a set of hymn-books, a number adequate to the largest mass meeting it is likely to hold. This will avoid the necessity of depending upon the singing books of the church where the union happens to meet, a different book each time, and not always suitable. Besides, the union will, of course, exercise the greatest care in choosing its song-book, and will make the selection a hint to the societies as to the best music.

In this connection a word should be said for the song-books published by the United Society of Christian Endeavor. These books are varied in contents, some of them presenting more popular music than others, but all of them excellent in words and music. They have been prepared by leading musicians with the special needs of our societies constantly before them. They are low in price, attractive in form, and have proved to be very useful in many thousands of societies. Loyalty to our national organization, whose only support is its publication department, should lead all unions and societies to examine its song-books before purchasing elsewhere, and to buy them if they prove to be the best.

Society Choirs.—The union music committee will make it part of its task to organize choirs in the various societies, seeing that each has a good leader and is doing good work for its society and church. To stimulate these choirs the union may devote a meeting largely to songs by the different choirs, a jury of musicians to give the award of a baton to the leader of the choir that does the best. The society choirs will also be used in the union mass meetings, taking turns in this service, and will be a strong feature of whatever concerts the union may give.

A Union Chorus.—Whatever the societies may do with their choirs, the union itself should have a chorus in which all the choirs will be united together, with as many other singers among the Endeavorers as can be persuaded to join. Insist upon regular attendance upon the rehearsals. Have an inspiring leader with a passion for the best music and a love for young people.

Make much of the union chorus at the union meetings. Let it be as large as possible, but remember that size is not necessary for the best results. Do the best you can with the numbers you can obtain, and those numbers will be sure to grow.

A Union Orchestra.—If the union music committee can find a good orchestra leader for the work, it will be easy in most towns to bring together enough young people who play different musical instruments to make a capital orchestra. Of course if the societies have orchestras in any considerable number, a very large orchestra can be brought together. The union orchestra will combine with the union choir in separate pieces, and will support the choir by its accompaniments.

Musical Loans.—The union music committee may constitute itself a musical exchange. It will learn about the interesting musical features developed in any society, and will bring about the loan of those features to the other societies of the union. If, for example, some society discovers a good soloist or a good player upon the violin, he or she will be asked to go to this society and that and give them solos, vocal or instrumental. The Endeavorer thus loaned will take part just as in his home society, and thus contribute doubly to the enjoyment and profit of his auditors. He will also on his return to his home society report the good methods he may have observed.

Union Concerts.—If all this musical work is going on, or even only a part of it, a union concert once a year will be inevitable. It should be prepared with the greatest care, and not advertised till it is thoroughly ready. It should be advertised well and an admission fee should be charged. The money will pay for the union music, for the services of the music leaders of the union, and perhaps will help out the general treasury.

Music in the Union Meetings.—While a union choir and orchestra will give special pieces at the union meetings, there will be an opportunity for solos, both vocal and instrumental, and congregational singing will not be neglected. The first is necessary for the training of young singers and musicians. Do not think it necessary to bring in adult and experienced singers for the union meetings, but remember that the union is for the discovery of the future musicians of the church and their training, as well as to do similar work for the church along other lines. Though the beginners in solo-singing will not, of course, do so well as the experienced singers you might introduce, yet the young people themselves will be more interested in the efforts of some from their own number than in the efficient work of older persons.

As to congregational singing in the union meetings, make this also educational. It will be samples of the best work that can be done in the societies, and especially it will show the society music leaders how to bring out the singing powers of their own members in their smaller meetings. Here, for example, will be practised the singing, first of the girls and then of the boys, first of the left side of the audience then of the right, the responsive singing of the main floor and the galleries, the singing of the stanzas by one society while the rest come in on the chorus, and many other variations on the ordinary singing. Here a sharp distinction will be made between the prayer songs and the hymns of triumph, the marching songs and the songs of solemn ecstasy. The methods used in the union meetings will be used in the societies, provided the union music committee sees that each society has its song leader and its choir with a vigorous music committee to keep them at work.

Musical Contests.—Union music committees will do much to promote music in the societies if they will organize musical contests. These may be of three kinds: singing by the individual societies, singing by society choirs, and playing by society orchestras. One night the first of these contests may be held, the next night the second, and the third night the third. The fourth night you may have a contest allowing the combination of orchestra and society, or orchestra and choir. The judges in making their awards should consider the size of the choir or orchestra in relation to its society; that is, a large society furnishing a small choir or orchestra should not receive so much honor as a small society furnishing a choir or orchestra of equal size, even if the quality of the music is equal.

The music committee will stimulate the plan by visits to the different societies, urging that they enter into the contest. See to the appointment of music committees in all the societies. Let each society appoint some leader of the singing, who will drill the society for a few minutes in each prayer meeting. Encourage home meetings for practice. Make the societies understand that the spirited singing of ordinary hymns will make a better result of the contest than the rendition of any unusual piece. Keep to the front the goal of practical usefulness.

A special public meeting of the union will have for its main feature the singing of the contesting societies or choirs or the playing of the contesting orchestras. Judges will be appointed—the most skilled musicians you can interest in the affair. The prize may be the classical one of wreaths of oak leaves placed upon the heads of the performers. If this public meeting is well advertised, it will be a great success. The address should treat the value of music in worship and should give practical suggestions with regard to it.

A most happy and appropriate outcome of the contest would be the formation of a union choir or orchestra made up of the combined musical forces of the societies.

Serving the Church with Union Music.—Sometimes the local churches have special needs which the union musical organizations, the union choir and orchestra, can meet. Some church, for instance, may entertain an important denominational society. The Presbytery may meet in some church, or the State association of the denomination. The churches may have a series of union evangelistic meetings. There may be a union temperance rally. If the director of the union music and the chairman of the union music committee keep their eyes and ears open, they will find many opportunities for service of the churches with the union singers and musicians. And every such service will not only help the churches but will promote the popularity and influence of Christian Endeavor.

Serving the Community with Union Music.—Sometimes the union music committee can use the union musical organization for the good of the community at large. For example, it may organize groups of singers who will go around the streets singing Christmas carols on Christmas morning. Similarly New Year's hymns may be sung on New Year's evening. Patriotic songs may be sung on the common on the Fourth of July, and the orchestra may play patriotic airs. Marching songs may be learned, and the Endeavorers may form a feature of civic parades. These services will depend largely upon the varying needs of the times, but a wide-awake union music committee will meet those needs as they arise.

Music in the State Union.—The musical work in county and district unions and in State unions will consist largely of seeing that the town and city unions have good music committees hard at work in the ways already described, and this may be brought about by the executive committees of the larger unions. Sometimes, however, it may be best to appoint music directors or superintendents for the larger unions, who will inspire the unions and societies over the wider area with their own musical enthusiasm. Such music superintendents, in co-operation with the local heads of the musical work, would have charge of the music of the county, district, and State conventions.

State Hymns.—It is not easy to obtain a good State Christian Endeavor hymn; and if the State has a poor one, every effort should be made to substitute one that is adequate. A State hymn should have inspiring words. It is abominable to force upon the young people mere doggerel and compel them to sing it as often as a State hymn must be sung. Moreover, the State hymn rep-

resents the society in a very conspicuous way, and if
it is crude in words and a mere jig in tune, Christian
Endeavor also is set down as crude and trivial. The
State executive committee should, if it is in doubt
about the State hymn, submit it to the judgment of a
committee of good musical and literary judges. If
they decide against it, then go to work and obtain a
hymn that will meet with their unqualified approval
both as to words and music. You may open a public
competition; though if you do this, see to it that the
best talent available takes part in the competition. It
is better usually to apply privately to poets and com-
posers well known to the committee of judges, and get
a State hymn from them. If the result is not just what
you want, keep on trying till you get it. Better no
State hymn at all than a poor one.

Music in the Conventions.—In the chapter on conventions this subject will be more fully treated. It will
suffice here to say that the convention music deserves
the very best efforts of convention committees, and that
the convention music committee should be made up of
experts. They should not, however, be pedantic, but
should have the spirit of youth ; and, while using only
the best music, should realize that the bounding enthusiasm of youth calls for something different from funeral
marches, though these are classics. The music of our
conventions should be an event in the higher life of all
present, and it may be made this if the convention
music committees are awake to their responsibilities
and opportunities.

Class Work on Chapter XVI

The Leader's Questions

Why should our union do musical work?

How should the union music committee be made up?

How will it conduct a conference?

How will it work to improve the society music?

How are neighborhood " sings " conducted?

How will a union singing school be managed?

Why should the union own its own hymn-books?

How will the union promote society choirs?

What are the advantages of a union chorus? a union orchestra?

How will the music committee promote " musical loans "?

How will union concerts be arranged?

How may the music of union meetings be improved?

How may musical contests be organized?

How will the union music help the churches?

To what community uses may the union music be put?

What musical work may be done in the State union?

Topic for a Talk or Essay

The Evangelistic Use of Music.

Subject for a Class Debate

Resolved, that poor singing in our societies is due to poor music books.

CHAPTER XVII

UNION PUBLICITY

The Importance of Publicity.—Almost all secular business depends upon advertising, and so does our Father's business. If we want people to be interested in any work we must tell them about it ; and once telling is not enough, we must remind them of it as long as we want their interest to continue. Gifts to missions have greatly increased since bright methods of telling the people about missions have been adopted. Interest in the temperance cause is tremendously promoted by the very able periodical and book literature on the subject. Christian Endeavor from the beginning has been wide-awake to the value of printer's ink, and has profited immensely from the use of it. The local societies can and should have their press committees, which will give what publicity they can to the work of the societies and the churches with which they are connected ; but a society working by itself along this line works at a great disadvantage. The papers will deal with a single representative of all the societies, but will not be bothered with a dozen representatives from a dozen separate societies. No one society can furnish a constant weekly bulletin of interest, but a dozen societies can fill such a bulletin with bright items without trouble. Publicity, therefore, is a legitimate union enterprise ; it is a task in which the co-operation of the societies is positively necessary.

Moreover, from the view-point of the education for the kingdom of God which Christian Endeavor carries on, this union press work is very important. Skilled publicity men will be of the greatest advantage to the church of the future; quite essential, in fact, if the church is to hold her own with secular forces. Nowhere can they be trained more efficiently than in this union press work. Therefore it is to be pushed for the sake not only of the present gains of the churches and their Christian Endeavor societies and the Christian Endeavor union, but even more for the sake of the future progress of the kingdom of God.

The Union Press Committee Organized.—For the chairman of the union press committee you must have a good executive who is systematic and ardent and can inspire others with his enthusiasm. He must be a good writer and must have some practical knowledge of newspaper work, or at least the ability to absorb such knowledge quickly. For his assistants on the committee you will obtain as many skilled workers as possible, gradually working in others for the sake of the training and to provide successors.

If the union is small the press committee will contain one representative from each society. He will naturally be the chairman of the society press committee, for such a committee will be organized in each society. If it is not already organized, the first work of the union press committee will be to see that every society has a press committee. If the union is too large for this, it will contain a member from each section of the city, who will be responsible for gathering the news of his section from his local press committees. These local press committees should not be large, but should usually be of more than one member, partly for the sake of the training and partly that the field may be more efficiently covered.

Systematize the Work.—The work of gathering and preparing the news of the week must go on with clock-like precision. On a certain day and at a certain time on that day each local press committee will hand its items to a section committeeman, who will hand them immediately to the chairman of the union committee. Of course, if there are no sectional divisions, the copy will go directly to the union chairman. The local workers will be so drilled in matter and method that their copy will require little or no editing, but can at once be sent to the papers.

Promptness and Timeliness.—The chairman must insist that there shall be no delay in this process. He must get his copy in on time. Newspapers cannot wait for any one, least of all will they wait for religious news. Promptness is not only a newspaper necessity but it is a valuable element in the drill.

Timeliness is equally necessary. Whatever is reported must have happened within a week if you are reporting for weeklies, or on the preceding day if you are reporting for a daily. There is nothing upon which a journalist looks with greater scorn than stale news. The minute after a thing has happened is the time for writing it up for the press. The next half-hour is the ideal time for sending it in !

What Topics to Treat.—The average person has no " news sense." He knows that he enjoys reading certain things and does not enjoy reading other things, but never stops to think what kind of matter each is. The born reporter has, by instinct or careful reasoning and observation, a knowledge of what will interest people. He knows, for instance, that while a list of the persons chosen for officers of a society will interest those persons greatly and will interest their immediate friends mildly, it will be the dullest kind of reading for every one else ; therefore he avoids such lists of officers as he would the plague. That, on the other hand, is precisely the material with which a person with no " nose for news " fills his column.

Nothing is more important in writing for the press than the selection of topics. This selection must be made with an eye to the paper for which you are writing. Personal items that are full of interest in a local paper, published where the parties are well known, would be quite barren of interest in a national paper. On the other hand, items regarding the society's relation to great national movements would be full of interest in the national paper, but would be of interest in a local paper only if accompanied by a careful explanation.

Therefore no rule for the choice of topics can be given, except that of imaginative sympathy. " Put yourself in his place," the place of your reader, and try to judge how the proposed topic would appeal to him. A bright writer can add interest to any topic, but his work is far more successful if he starts with a topic in which the reader's interest is assured.

Young writers for the press are often advised to study the paper for which they write and send it such paragraphs as it is in the habit of printing. If, however, the paper is filled with trifling personal gossip, the religious reporter will make a mistake if he imitates its contents. What advantage comes to the kingdom of God from an addition to the number of such paragraphs? Our Christian Endeavor items must rise above personal gossip, or it is not worth while troubling ourselves and the editors with them. Let the Christian Endeavor reporter consider the actual work of his society. What is it doing that is really worth while? This is what is to be reported. Of course, if it is novel, so much the better, though we must remember that much religious work that is perfectly familiar to church people is a novelty to those that do not go to church. New methods are always worth reporting. So are all worthy achievements. The best item from the newspaper view-point is one that pictures in a fresh way some original and striking deed. These, however, are not to be recorded every day, while faithful effort and faithful accomplishment may be reported right along. It is the business of the press committee to report it in a readable way.

How to Write the News.—The very first rule for young writers is, " Be simple." Affected, pompous, pretentious writing is always out of place, but especially is such writing on the simple themes that are treated by Christian Endeavor correspondents.

The second rule is, " Be clear." See that your sentences mean one thing and only one. Do not invert your sentences or leave out the little words that belong in them.

The third rule is, " Be brief." This does not mean that you are to squeeze the juice out of your items, but that you are to say your say straightforwardly, and, having said it, stop. Omit the introduction, cut out unnecessary explanations, and leave off the comment at the close. Just give the news. Your readers prefer to think their own thoughts about it, and not yours.

The fourth rule is, " Be bright." A bit of fun is always good news. A snappy, unusual way of putting things is a boon to any paper. Every touch of originality and freshness that you can introduce will make your manuscript doubly welcome.

The fifth rule—it should really stand first for many reasons—is, " Be accurate." Be sure of your facts. Make every detail exact. Do not guess at figures. Spell proper names just as they should be spelled, and print them out unless your penmanship is as plain as print, or unless—better still—you are using a typewriter. When you make an editor print a correction in the next number, you have about destroyed your hold upon him and his paper.

Set before you the best models, which you will find in the leading papers. Study them carefully and often. Go over thoughtfully every bit of manuscript you send in, trying to improve it. Study your writings after they appear in print, and do not rest satisfied unless your work shows a decided improvement week after week. Writing is a difficult art, and all writing on religious themes or for the sake of the church is of the utmost importance. Seek to do your very best.

The Preparation of Copy.—Most editors insist upon typewritten copy. If you can get a typewriter, learn to use it. The final copy sent in by the chairman of the union committee should be typewritten always, though the copy as received from the local writers need only be written very clearly. Where the same material is sent to several papers it may be manifolded, but every copy should be clear. Some papers call for copy furnished to them alone. In that case, different members of the union press committee will be assigned to the different papers of the city, each studying the requirements of the paper to which he is assigned and seeking to meet these requirements. Of course the same news from the societies will be open to all these special reporters.

In the preparation of copy, note carefully the right way to make the paragraph, and put ample space between the different paragraphs of a disconnected series. Refer to the dictionary constantly for spelling and compounding. Learn the right use of the comma, semicolon, and colon. Look out for your quotation marks. Capitalize properly. Always keep an exact copy of your items and compare it with the printed result, noting the errors which the editor had to correct and the changes he made in the sentences, so that you will not make these mistakes in the future. Upon your care in these particulars will depend much of your progress, and your increase in value to the paper.

Getting into the Papers.—Of course our Christian Endeavor press committees will not expect to be paid for their work. They will be glad to get their items printed without pay. And generally the editors will be glad to print them, provided they are of the right sort. Any editor, however, knowing how rare is the news sense together with the ability to write clearly and brightly, will look with suspicion upon the offer of a set of amateurs to furnish copy for his paper. Do not propose at the start a regular Christian Endeavor department. Merely send in your items, and let the editor use what he pleases and print them where he pleases. Be grateful at first, and a little surprised, if a single one out of perhaps two dozen items appears in print. Be willing to serve your apprenticeship. If you know the editor personally, you may be able to arrange with him for regular correspondence, getting his advice regarding its nature and especially learning from him just when it should be sent in. If you have not this personal acquaintance, simply send the news by mail, addressing it not to him but to the paper. If you do your work well, space will be made for it gradually, and as fast as the editor becomes convinced of its value. Your success in getting in will depend solely upon your skill in preparing interesting and vital news and sending it to him in the right shape. Personal influence has nothing to do with it. " Bulldozing " methods will not work. Persistent calling will have no effect—at least, no favorable effect. Nothing will win the day for the press committee except journalistic ability. And that you can gain if you will.

Christian Endeavor Departments in Secular Papers.—The secular papers will in time be willing to give you regular space for Christian Endeavor departments if you prove your ability to make them interesting—genuine " circulation-feeders." You will put into these departments every week the most important doings of the societies and of the churches, and the most interesting news about the progress of Christian Endeavor in the world field. Generally comments on the Christian Endeavor prayer-meeting topics will not be wanted, as most papers that use them at all obtain them from the syndicates.

Christian Endeavor in the Religious Weeklies.— The papers published by the different denominations require a different treatment from that accorded the secular papers. For the purpose of reaching the religious weeklies the press committee will divide itself denominationally. The representatives of the Presbyterian societies, for instance, will constitute a Presbyterian section. They will gather all the news they can from the Presbyterian churches and societies in the union, and after they have brought together a little budget of the most newsy items—not waiting till they become stale—they will send them off to the denominational papers. Church news will be included with the Christian Endeavor news, and thus the committee will do the widest service for their churches as well as their societies. In this work the interests of the larger field must be borne in mind. Remember that those readers do not care for local personalities, but want to hear about whatever is of general interest.

What " The Christian Endeavor World " Wants. —I know very well the kind of news *The Christian Endeavor World* is eager to print, and a description of it will indicate what news every other paper wants, after proper account is taken of the differences in constituency. As our national Christian Endeavor paper goes all over the world and to all parts of America, it cannot take room for items that are of interest only locally. It cannot print a line that is put in to satisfy personal ambition or to please some influential local Endeavorer. To be sure, it would help the paper to gain the approval of such persons, but it must be gained by other means, if at all.

So, first, *The Christian Endeavor World* wants news while it is news. Correspondents that tarry till the convention report is printed in some weekly paper or

even in pamphlet form and then send us that are of no
earthly use to us. If the convention report is mailed
to us, as it should be, the very day after the close of
the convention, even then, on account of our large
editions and widely extended circulation, it will be
three weeks before the report can reach our sub-
scribers.

In the convention report we want few names and
few subjects of addresses—only what is vital. If a
bright new topic is treated, we want to know it. If a
widely-known speaker takes part, tell us. If an ob-
scure speaker gets off a striking sentence, quote it. If
a new convention method is tried, describe it. Anything that is fresh and interesting and helpful; nothing
that is routine, commonplace, and dull.

The same is true of the reports of society and union
work. We are sometimes charged with neglecting
certain States or cities or countries in our news page.
The charge is absurd. It is to our interest and the
interest of the Christian Endeavor cause that every city
and State and country should receive full and frequent
mention. But not unless the real news is sent us. We
are all the time trying to get it, but we do not always
succeed. I am quite safe in saying that no piece of
vital, interesting news was ever sent us and failed to
get into print. We may have had to condense a thousand words into a hundred; but the essence of it was
given, and given with all desirable fulness. Like all
other editors, we must be the judge of that; and it is
in every way to our interest to judge wisely.

These remarks would doubtless receive the hearty
assent of every editor for whom our press committees
write, as applied to their respective papers. Nothing
is more unmanly than the whine of a writer who fails

to get by an editor's blue pencil. Nothing is easier than to charge him with stupid carelessness or prejudice. And nothing, in the vast majority of cases, is more foolish than such a charge.

Press-Committee Scrap-books.—The chairman of the press committee or one of the members of the committee will make clippings of everything written by the committee which is published, and will paste it all in chronological order in a committee scrap-book, marking each clipping with the name of the paper that printed it. This scrap-book will be of great value to the committee in judging of their progress in the work, and will be most useful as a guide to following committees, to whom it should be handed down. There will be a place in the scrap-book for all the advertising material which the committee gets out— whatever it does in the way of publicity.

The Union Advertising.—This may well be placed in the hands of the press committee, and in that case the name, "Publicity Committee," would be more appropriate. The committee will prepare the posters for the union mass meetings, or the handbills, which may be distributed from house to house or sent through the mail. Some of these will be placed upon the town bulletin boards and the bulletin boards of the churches. Posters may be placed in shop-windows. Circulars may be written describing various special operations of the union, such as its hospital work. Notices may be sent to the pastors for reading in the pulpit and insertion in the church papers or church calendars. Indeed, the scope of the union press committee may be greatly extended if it also attends to the general publicity of the union.

Local Christian Endeavor Papers.—The union press committee may conduct the union bulletin or local Christian Endeavor paper, if it is thought wise to publish one. In that case a member of the committee will be appointed editor, and will have this as his particular province, aided by the other members of the committee as he calls upon them. A four- or eight-page monthly entirely devoted to the work of the union may be supported by advertisements in most unions. A State union can support a larger paper by subscriptions, but care should be taken to begin on a very small scale and increase the size of the paper only gradually and never beyond the certain income of the sheet. A very few unions have made the State paper a source of profit; far more have incurred heavy losses on account of foolishly ambitious newspaper enterprises. Generally speaking, the most sensible publication is merely a printed bulletin with no advertisements and no subscription list, printed when the need for it arises and sent free through the mail at full postage rates. Three or four times a year will usually be a frequent enough issue of the little news-letter or bulletin, which thus becomes a valuable adjunct to the union publicity at little trouble or expense.

Convention Press Committees.—The State and national Christian Endeavor conventions require much publicity both beforehand and afterwards if they are to be successful. The convention press committee should consist of seasoned workers from the union of the convention city. It should get to work as early as possible; indeed, as soon as the convention city is chosen. If it is a State convention, its field is the papers of the State, and sometimes those of adjoining States; but if it is a national convention, its field is as wide as the nation. Special articles about the convention will be written for the more important papers, and frequent printed bulletins will be sent out to all the papers. Care should be taken to make these bulletins really interesting, otherwise the editors will not use them. Short paragraphs are the best form. Use only the essential details of time and place. Pack the bulletins full of the facts that will interest the average reader. Use anecdotes of the more striking speakers, and possibly their portraits. Use brisk sentences relating to the more striking subjects to be treated. Describe in snappy sentences the unique and unusual features of the convention. If you include items about the same fact in successive bulletins, get different persons to write them and make them as different as possible.

With all this publicity will go attractive posters for society bulletin boards and shop-windows, "stickers" for the backs of envelopes, circulars for corresponding secretaries, and every other kind of advertisement that the committee can devise.

Then, during the convention the press committee will see that the local papers keep reporters in attendance on the session and will care for their comfort, furnishing them with particulars about the speakers and with other facts about the work. If possible, arrange with the editors to treat the convention editorially at some time during the session.

Immediately after the convention send out over the State a well-written brief account of the gathering, which many county and town papers will publish. During the convention see that the Associated Press sends an item about it to the metropolitan dailies. Urge the local press committees over the State to introduce items regarding it into their local columns. Encourage echo meetings of the delegates, and distribute before the convention is over a printed plan for a bright echo meeting, giving an outline of the convention under headings that may be used as subjects by a succession of speakers at the echo meetings. The convention press committee has much to do toward rendering permanent the results of the gathering.

Class Work on Chapter XVII

The Leader's Questions

How is publicity valuable in the work of a Christian Endeavor union ?

How is the union press committee organized ?

What features of the work should be emphasized ?

What topics should the committee treat ?

How should the news be written ?

How should copy be prepared ?

How can the committee get into the papers ?

What work should be done in the secular papers ? in the religious weeklies ?

What does *The Christian Endeavor World* want ?

What will the committee scrap-book contain ?

What union advertising will the committee attend to ?

When are local Christian Endeavor papers useful ?

What is the work of a convention press committee ?

Topic for a Talk or Essay

Publicity Pays.

Subject for a Class Debate

Resolved, that our union should print a monthly bulletin.

CHAPTER XVIII

THE UNION LITERATURE COMMITTEE

Why a Union Literature Committee?—Every society should have a literature committee (or a "good-
literature committee," as it is commonly called, though
the "good" should be superfluous among Christian
Endeavorers!) and one of the first duties of the union
literature committee is to see that similar committees
are appointed in the societies. This of itself would
warrant the appointment of the union literature committee, at least till the societies had their committees at
work. And there is much that a union literature committee may do that society committees cannot do.
There is need of a central bureau for this work, to give
information and to focus and strengthen effort. Few
unions have literature committees, but all should form
them.

The Make-up of the Committee.—The chairman of
the union literature committee will be a young man or
young woman who knows much about books and
periodicals, whose taste is well developed, whose
sympathies are wide, and who is a good executive.
The rest of the committee may consist of the chairmen
of the society literature committees. There will be
work for a large committee if the suggestions given below are carried out.

The Literature-Committee Conference.—Hold this
conference early in the society year, or at least as soon

as most of the societies have formed literature committees. Bring together all the members of these committees. Open the meeting by an earnest talk on the value of good books and papers. This talk should be given by the best speaker you can find, one in love with the subject, but also one who can confine his words on this fascinating theme to fifteen minutes. Follow this with an open discussion of the work of the literature committee in the societies, as outlined in the United Society's pamphlet on this committee, including many questions and answers. Discuss also the literature work of the union, and show how the society literature committees may aid it.

The Union Literature Exchange.—Every union should establish a union literature exchange, whose work is to learn where good reading matter that has been used may have further use, and keep a list of these addresses ready for the societies. The literature exchange will investigate each address and make sure that good use is made of all reading matter sent there. The literature exchange will also learn how papers and books should be sent, and give this information to the societies. Union literature exchanges should be in communication, so that an address found by one union to be all right may be passed on to other unions with full information regarding it, thus greatly simplifying the work. These lists will be changed from time to time, and when one address for any reason is no longer to be used, a statement to this effect should be sent to the other union literature exchanges, with the reason for dropping the name. The union literature exchange should be a permanency, and may consist of only one Endeavorer reappointed year after year. This is good work for some shut-in Endeavorer who is faithful to little details.

A United Society Agency.—The union literature committee should be a regular and active agency for the sale of the books and pamphlets on Christian Endeavor methods published by the United Society of Christian Endeavor, as well as the official pins, badges, pennants, and other helps for the inspiring of the Endeavorers. The members of the committee should all have copies of the United Society's catalogue, and the committee should keep on hand samples of everything in the United Society's stock. These samples should be exhibited at every meeting of the union and orders taken. A number of copies of all the most popular articles should be on hand ready for immediate sale. Through the society literature committees the sale of new helps will be further pushed in the local societies. This feature of the work is most important, not only to the United Society, whose existence depends upon the profits of its publication department, but also to the societies of the union, whose good work depends upon their learning the best methods which are so fully described in the publications of the United Society.

An Agency for "The Christian Endeavor World."— The international Christian Endeavor organ is as necessary to the work as the publications of the United Society. It prints the doings of the societies and unions all over the world, and gives the first news of the large plans of the United Society. In its pages appear first all the most helpful methods of work. At the same time, with its prayer-meeting helps, its inspiring articles, poems, and stories, and its many admirable departments, it is a great blessing to the private life of every reader. The union literature committee, working through the society literature committees, should see that every society has a large club for *The Christian Endeavor World*, and that the club is kept up year after year. The cash commission and many premiums given for new subscriptions may become a union asset of considerable value if the union does not give the premium advantage to the societies.

Other Periodicals.—The union literature committee will promote the subscription lists of the local and State Christian Endeavor papers, if there are any, and will do what it can toward obtaining subscriptions for the denominational papers, though here the denominational committee, if you have one, will be most active. One day may well be set apart as " Religious Paper Day." a thorough canvass being made on that day for the various religious papers—Christian Endeavor, denominational, and interdenominational.

Gather Up the Papers and Magazines.—The union literature committee through the society committees will systematically gather up all the thousands of good papers and magazines which have been read in the homes of the Endeavorers and their friends, and which would ordinarily be burned up or thrown away. These should be put where they will do good, and the places for them are very numerous. They may be placed in weather-proof receptacles on the backs of park seats. They may be put into barber shops, replacing or counteracting some of the worthless reading matter usually found there. In suitable receptacles (all these receptacles will bear the name of the Christian Endeavor union) they will be placed in the hotels, the railroad stations, the police stations, the fire-department stations, the old ladies' homes, orphans' homes, poorhouses, prisons, hospitals, asylums—indeed, in every place where experience proves that they will be well used. They may be sent on board ship. They may be placed in army posts and in navy yards. They may be sent to lumber camps, where they will be read with eagerness. The missionaries will be glad to have them, for missionary salaries afford small sums for subscriptions; and when the missionary has read them, he will know of others that will appreciate them. It is a sin to throw away food for the body when there are so many hungry people in the world, and it is an equal sin to throw away food for the mind.

The literature committee will have regular days, once a month, or oftener, when the society committees will gather up this reading matter and bring it to some central place where it will be sorted, made up into bundles, and taken to these various institutions.

Gather Up the Books.—In the same way that the literature committee brings together the papers and magazines which have been read and are no longer wanted, it will gather up the old books and put them to good new uses. Careful discrimination must be exercised here, since bad books sometimes get even into Christian homes, and Christian Endeavor must not give them further circulation; but most of the books will be clean and well worth passing along. The committee will sort them—some for the young people in the libraries of mission Sunday schools, some for the sailors, some for missionaries, and so on. Every book should carry a label saying that it comes from your Christian Endeavor union with the good will of the young people.

Libraries.—The union literature committee will further the formation of Christian Endeavor libraries by the societies. These libraries will consist of books on Christian Endeavor methods, together with the pamphlets and leaflets for the different committees and lines of work ready to lend to the successive officers and committee chairmen. There will also be books on the history of Christian Endeavor, on temperance, on missions, and on the history of your denomination. Society librarians will be appointed, and the society collections will be kept up by the addition of the latest Christian Endeavor literature.

The union also will have a Christian Endeavor library full of books on Christian Endeavor, especially for lending to societies that have no libraries and to ministers that wish to study the Christian Endeavor work. The union lookout committee will find this library very useful. A union librarian may be appointed who will take charge of the union library and who will once a year hold a conference of the society librarians.

The union will also further the use of the public library by noting the best religious books in it and sending lists of them now and then to the societies, particularly mentioning those books that fit in with the current prayer-meeting topics, not forgetting the missionary and temperance topics, unless the union missionary and temperance committees do this work for themselves. The library authorities will be glad to have suggestions now and then of new Christian Endeavor books which should be in the public library. Sometimes the public library will lend little collections of books, perhaps fifty at a time, to societies that will make a business of reading them and then of exchanging them for fifty more, just as certain libraries do this for Sunday schools.

Many towns have no library at all, and in these the union literature committee may start a movement for a public library. Get the influential citizens back of you if you can. Receive subscriptions for the purchase of books. Get as many persons as possible to donate books. Have a committee of well-known readers and scholars appointed for passing on the books to be admitted. If you cannot get a special room for the library, have it kept in a private house. Let the Endeavorers take turns acting as librarian for a few hours each day. You will be surprised to see how rapidly and easily the books come in, and how interested people will be in the plan as soon as it is started.

Reading Bulletins.—It will aid the Endeavorers in their reading if the union literature committee gets different Endeavorers to read the various prominent periodicals, one apiece, reporting to the committee chairman the best things in each number. A bulletin containing this information may be duplicated and sent to the societies for posting on their bulletin boards. Worth-while books will also be named, with, in each case, the name of the Endeavorer who vouches for the book.

The Use of Clippings.—The union literature committee will do a good deed if it interests the societies, through their literature committees, in the collecting of clippings on various subjects. These clippings may be pasted in scrap-books, one for each subject, or they may be placed in a series of envelopes, each for a subject. Each committee will have an envelope or a scrap-book, and there will be an envelope for each prominent religious theme likely to be treated in the prayer meeting, such as prayer, patience, the Bible, Sunday, courage, Christmas, Easter, patriotism.

Interesting collections of clippings, poetry and prose, may be made for hospitals and mounted upon light cards easy for sick folks to handle.

The Use of Tracts.—The union literature committee may get a supply of helpful gospel tracts, and persuade the societies to purchase them and give them away. Each member will take a few and see that they are placed where they will do the most good and will be read. Once a year, at some appropriate meeting, call for the recital of experiences connected with these tracts.

Reading Courses.—One of the best ways to set the Endeavorers to reading good books is through the offer of some reward for the best and longest list of books read by any Endeavorer of the union in a specified time, say three months. You will appoint a committee of advice on good books, those being chosen that are accessible to the Endeavorers. The Endeavorers may form their own courses, and they may be largely fiction (but it must be of the best), or largely of something better than fiction, as history and biography.

Reading circles may be formed throughout the union with the aid of the union literature committee. The committee will suggest the plan to the societies, will tell its many advantages, and will name a few interesting and wise books that are good to read aloud ; books, for instance, like Mary Antin's " The Promised Land."

Class Work on Chapter XVIII

The Leader's Questions

Why should our union have a literature committee?

How should the committee be made up?

How will a literature-committee conference be conducted?

What is the work of a union literature exchange?

What is the work of a United Society agency? of an agency for *The Christian Endeavor World?* for other periodicals?

How will the literature committee collect good reading matter?

How will the literature committee promote the formation of Christian Endeavor libraries?

What will the committee do with reading bulletins?

How will the committee use clippings?

How will the committee promote the use of tracts?

How will the committee promote the use of reading courses?

Topic for a Talk or Essay

Read Only the Best.

Subject for a Class Debate

Resolved, that our union should establish a Christian Endeavor library.

CHAPTER XIX

UNION WORK FOR JUNIORS AND INTERMEDIATES

When Should We Have a Junior Union?—Not many cities have formed Junior unions, and far more should have them than are enjoying them now. Most cities that can support a union of the Young People's societies have enough Junior societies to form a successful union; and even where the Junior societies are few, if there is a union of the older societies, the few Junior societies may well unite. Their joint efforts should be exerted for a while mainly toward the formation of new Junior societies, thus strengthening the Junior union and the cause of Christian Endeavor at the same time. By all means form a Junior union.

Relation between the Two Unions.—At the start the Young People's union will aid the Junior union and be very closely connected with it. The older union will appoint a Junior superintendent, who, with a committee from the older union, will form a Junior union. He or she will probably become the first president of the Junior union. The Junior union president will be a member *ex officio* of the executive committee of the older union, and the older union will help the Junior union financially and with advice and moral support till it is well established. Later, of course, the two unions will become more independent of each other, but always the president of the Junior union should be

195

a member of the executive committee of the Young People's union, and make reports to the latter union as an officer of it. The two unions will hold a joint meeting at least once a year, and they may co-operate in much of their committee work, such as the work for hospitals, the country week, and the work for the poor.

The Organization of the Junior Union.—The Junior union will have a full set of officers and many of the same committees that are found in the older union, such as the lookout committee, the missionary committee, the social committee, the music committee, and, of course, the executive committee. The officers of the Junior union will be mainly the Junior superintendents, and all of these superintendents may belong to the executive committee. You will do well, however, to place upon the union committees (not as chairmen of course) a number of the oldest and brightest of the Juniors themselves, thus initiating them into the work and developing their powers for larger activities. You will be surprised to see how much the Juniors can do even of this wide and outreaching work.

Junior Superintendents' Conferences. — Whether they are held under the auspices of the older union and its Junior superintendent, or you have a Junior union and they are held under its auspices, every town with two or more Junior societies should have frequent conferences of the superintendents. The assistant superintendents will also come, of course; and if some societies are managed by Junior committees from the Young People's societies, these committees also will attend the conference.

It is well to close each conference with a general discussion of all points that the superintendents want to bring up ; but each conference should centre about some large theme connected with the conduct of the Junior society, such as how to keep order, how to interest the children in missions, and how to get the children to speak out of their own religious experiences. The topic will be opened by some superintendent of ability and knowledge, and then others will speak and there will be a genuine give and take of thought and experience. If a social hour with light refreshments closes the conference, it will bring the superintendents close together and greatly promote the interchange of thought. These conferences may well be held as often as once a month during the fall, winter, and spring. The older Juniors should sometimes be invited, those whom the superintendents think they can develop into superintendents. They will imbibe from the conferences much of the spirit of Junior work and many of the best principles and methods.

The Junior Union Lookout Committee.—If the Junior union is formed, it should relieve the lookout committee of the older union of the task of forming new Junior societies, since the superintendents of the Junior societies already formed are the best persons to advocate the extension of such work and establish new societies. They can go to the pastors, and especially the pastors' wives, and the heads of the Sunday-school primary departments, and can show them what an advantage a Junior society would be to the church and to all connected with the church. They can bring the children together in a bright meeting and tell them what the Junior society is and does, and draw them all into the new organization on the spot. They can lay their hands upon some young woman or young man who will become the first superintendent, or they can get the Young People's society to appoint a Junior committee to conduct the Junior society. And they can stand by the new society with advice and much practical aid till it is well on its feet. The Junior union lookout committee will not feel that its work is done till it has formed a Junior society in every church that has a Young People's society—and in other places as well, such as orphans' homes and in rural communities.

Junior Intervisitation.—The lookout committee of the Junior union may arrange a system of intervisitation like that of the older union. Delegates will be appointed by each society to visit some other society every week and report to their home society the following Sunday, telling the most interesting things they saw and heard. Two may go from each Junior society, and one of the two will be an older girl or boy. One or both of these will take part in the meeting they visit. The union committee will arrange the schedule so that each society will send a delegation and receive a delegation every night as long as the series of visits lasts.

Junior Outings.—The Junior union social committee will find its chief service to be the planning and management of outings in which all the Junior societies will share. These may be union picnics or trolley rides or walks or boat rides or excursions on the railways. They will have worth-while aims, such as a visit to some famous place or to become familiar with the different kinds of trees and flowers. Union sports will be planned, such as a series of athletic contests. Each superintendent will care for her own society, but all will join in the plans for the day. One result should be a better acquaintance of the Juniors of different churches and denominations.

Junior Exhibits.—The lookout committee of the Junior union will be of great service to the superintendents if it gathers up from each superintendent the best methods she has used so far as these can be illustrated by objects, charts, maps, etc. The collection will be exhibited at every superintendents' conference. The member of the lookout committee who has the exhibit in charge will understand the use of every object in it, and be glad to explain. Keep the exhibit fresh, and constantly urge the superintendents to add to it their very best ideas.

Form Junior Committees.—In all this work the union lookout committee will be confronted with the difficulty of obtaining Junior superintendents ; and here comes in the fine plan of substituting for the Junior superintendent, where such a person cannot be found, a Junior committee from the Young People's society, whose members will divide the work of a Junior superintendent among them. Out of these Junior committees in time many superintendents will be developed, but in the meantime the Junior societies will get along quite as well as under a single superintendent, and perhaps better. The Young People's society will be more interested in the Juniors, and will aid them in many ways. If the union lookout committee will only lay the cause of the children upon the consciences of the Endeavorers, it will not be hard to form these Junior committees. One member of the committee will preside over the Junior meetings, another will give chalk talks, another will conduct the committee work, another will run the socials, another will see to the music, another will keep order, etc. Whatever each knows best and can do best will be contributed to the Junior society.

Pastors and Churches Interested in Junior Work.— The union lookout committee can do much to interest pastors and churches in forming Junior societies and maintaining them when formed. Accounts of the work of the best Junior societies may be prepared and sent to the pastors and church officers. An exhibit of Junior work may be arranged for the ministers' meetings. Calls may be made upon the pastors to explain Junior work and answer questions. The Junior superintendent should have a place *ex officio* upon the church governing board, and the church should receive regular reports from her, and should support her work and see that it is kept up as steadily and faithfully as it cares for the work of the Sunday school.

A Junior Union Literature Agency.—The Junior union will have a committee, called perhaps the literature committee, whose special work it will be to keep on hand samples of all the United Society's helps for Junior workers and take orders for them. These helps will include the books and pamphlets of methods, the various cards, pins, mottoes, flags—everything, in fact, which the Junior workers need to carry on their work. The latest material will be on exhibition always at the superintendents' conferences. Be sure to include in this work the introduction of *The Junior Christian Endeavor World* and getting up clubs for it in every Junior society.

Superintendents' Round Robins.—The superintendents may be interested in writing out their experiences and reading the written experiences of others. Many will take part in this written work who are too retiring to take part freely in conferences. The letters will be bunched and sent to the superintendents in regular succession. As the round robin comes to each superintendent she will read the letters, remove her own letter from the bundle and substitute a new one, then send the letters along to the superintendent next on the list.

Mothers' Societies.—A fine work for the Junior lookout committee is the formation of mothers' societies of Christian Endeavor. Few churches have any mothers' meetings, and yet no type of religious gathering is more likely to be helpful. The monthly meeting of the Mothers' Society of Christian Endeavor has for its purpose to pray for the children of the mothers there gathered and to talk about their welfare. Talks will be given by the wisest persons available, and these will be followed by free questions and answers. The United Society has a ten-cent pamphlet giving full plans for mothers' societies, with a large number of programmes for their meetings. Such societies, of course, would be of the greatest assistance to the Junior superintendents and to the Junior societies.

Juniors in the Meetings of the Older Union.—The older societies will be led to take a greater interest in the work for the children if the Juniors are brought occasionally to the meetings of the older union and given some part in the programme. They may offer a series of sentence prayers, they may sing some songs by themselves, they may give little reports of their society work, they may present some exercise that will greatly please the audience. By all this the Juniors will be made interested in the older union, so that they will enter its work when they grow old enough for it.

The Public Meetings of the Junior Union.—The Juniors will have mass meetings of their own, not so often as the older union, but at least once a year. At the mass meeting of the Junior union there will be a talk by some one especially good at talking to children —best, a talk illustrated in some way. The Juniors themselves, however, will contribute the greater part of the programme—songs, recitations, exercises of many kinds. Each superintendent may contribute the best thing her society has done during the past months; it may be some missionary exercise or some Bible drill or some unusual song. The societies will take especial interest in a programme chiefly made up of child speakers.

A Junior Union Chorus.—The union will have a music committee, which will not only try to stimulate the music of the Junior societies but will build up a large chorus of the Juniors themselves, the best singers in all the societies. This chorus will be carefully drilled, and will be brought into the meetings of the older union to add to the programme. Of course all this training will help the music in the Junior societies.

Junior Union Ministries.—Many kinds of work in which Juniors engage need co-operation for their greatest effectiveness, and this co-operation can be arranged by the Junior union. For instance, the societies can take turns singing at the hospitals, they can unite in the work of giving Christmas presents to prisoners and to the children of the poor, and they can join in giving country weeks to poor children, especially if the union is in a country town.

Junior Union Study Classes.—Once a year the Junior superintendents may meet under an experienced leader for the study of some book on child training, or for Bible study, or for the study of civics, or for the study of one of the books in the Junior missionary series. Whatever the study is, it should be one that contributes directly to the work the superintendents are doing.

The Junior Union at Work for Temperance.—Some towns have made good use of the children in arousing temperance sentiment at election times, and Junior Endeavorers have done much to win temperance victories at the polls. The children can form a very effective temperance procession, carrying banners that cannot fail to move the voters. They can distribute temperance appeals at the doors of the homes. They can help in a poster campaign. They can form a chorus for the singing of temperance songs at mass meetings. All of this work is far better done under union management than when left to the separate societies.

Intermediate Societies and the Union.—All that has been said about Junior societies and the union of Young People's societies applies as well to Intermediate societies. The union will have an Intermediate superintendent, who will stimulate the Intermediate societies already existing and especially will see to the formation of new societies. Many fine societies have been formed in high schools, and boys and girls of that age are the best Intermediate material. As these new societies increase, an Intermediate union may be formed along the same lines as the older union and the Junior union. Conferences of Intermediate superintendents will be held, and the Intermediates, on account of their greater age, will be of even more assistance to the older union than the Juniors can be. The Intermediates come into the Christian Endeavor work at an age when the young people are developing very fast, and are likely to fall out of religious activities if they are not looked after with especial care. Most churches that can support a Young People's society and a Junior society can have also with great profit an Intermediate society. The boys and girls of high-school age are much better if in Intermediate societies than in their Junior or Young People's societies, and are much more likely to develop into strong workers. Our unions should not fail to push the Intermediate work. Few enterprises will be more profitable.

The Union Junior Superintendent.—Where a Junior union is not formed, the Junior superintendent of the union will try to do all that might be accomplished by the Junior union if it existed, all the while looking ahead to the time when a Junior union may be possible. The Junior superintendent of the union will visit the Junior societies, making friends of the superintendents, learning their successes, helping them out of their difficulties, talking briefly and inspiringly to the Juniors, and always leaving the work stronger than she found it. Once a month, if possible, she will conduct a Junior superintendents' conference. She will bring the Juniors together in bright union meetings, even if there is no Junior union. She will pick out the brightest of the superintendents to be her assistant and in time her successor. And all of this applies precisely to the Intermediate superintendent when this officer is appointed.

The State Junior and Intermediate Superintendents.

—These officers do for the Junior and Intermediate work at large what the local Junior and Intermediate union superintendents do for the work locally. They promote the appointment of Junior and Intermediate superintendents in the unions of the State, and the forming of Junior and Intermediate local unions. They organize campaigns for the forming of new Junior and Intermediate societies. They spread broadcast information about new methods of work. They correspond with the workers, answering questions, giving advice, and learning all the best ways of working. They make a collection of illustrative objects and of helpful books and pamphlets, and exhibit this collection in the State conventions. They gather statistics of the Junior and Intermediate societies from the local leaders. In many other ways suggested by the developing work they promote Junior and Intermediate Christian Endeavor.

Juniors and Intermediates at the State Convention.

—Our State conventions usually give up one session to the children, this being in charge of the State Junior superintendent working in conjunction with the local Junior superintendents. The children present some bright exercises which they have prepared very carefully for months in advance. They give songs and recitations, and some good speaker addresses them. It is well to make these Junior

sessions educational in relation to Junior work. They
should exhibit the best methods of work, and in so
doing they will please the audience as much as by
presenting some spectacle. One of the most effective
Junior exercises I have ever seen, for instance, was the
concert repetition of the parable of the sower, perfectly
shown by a large body of Juniors speaking in absolute
unison and with appropriate gestures beautifully made.
One of the most pleasing exercises ever given at a
national convention was a presentation of scenes in the
life of Livingstone made by a set of Junior boys who
had been studying the life of the great missionary. If
the Juniors have an orchestra or a chorus, or both, let
these be utilized in the convention. In short, make the
Junior hour an exhibit of the best work done by and
for the children during the year, and it will stimulate
to still better work all over the State in the year to
come.

Class Work on Chapter XIX

The Leader's Questions

When is a Junior union needed ?

What should be the relation between the Junior and
the Young People's unions ?

How will the Junior union be organized ?

How will Junior superintendents' conferences be
carried on ?

What is the work of the Junior union lookout committee ?

How is Junior intervisitation arranged ?

What kinds of Junior outings may be planned ?

What Junior exhibits may be made ?

How will Junior committees be formed in the Young People's societies?

How may pastors and churches be interested in Junior work?

What is the work of a Junior union literature agency?

What are superintendents' round robins?

How may mothers' societies be formed?

How will Juniors be used in the meetings of the older union?

What kinds of meetings will the Junior union hold?

What is the work of a Junior union chorus?

What large work can a Junior union do?

When will an Intermediate union be advisable?

When will a union Junior or Intermediate superintendent be appointed?

Describe Junior and Intermediate work in a State union.

Topic for a Talk or Essay

Our Responsibility for the Children.

Subject for a Class Debate

Resolved, that the formation of a Junior union in our city would promote Christian Endeavor.

CHAPTER XX

THE INTRODUCTION COMMITTEE

The Work of the Committee.—When Endeavorers remove from one town to another they are likely to drop out of the society work and even out of church work. If they do not at once fall in with active Endeavorers, they will be under the necessity of looking up a society for themselves, and many are too bashful or indifferent to do this. Many also are ignorant regarding the city, and do not know how to obtain for themselves an invitation to join a Christian Endeavor society. The work of the union introduction committee is to make it reasonably certain that Endeavorers removing from one place to another are heartily welcomed by the Endeavorers of their new home, put at once into touch with a society of their denomination, and settled promptly in a cordial and helpful church home. This is a very important task. Upon the way in which it is performed may depend the future welfare or failure of a life.

How Large Should the Committee Be?—An introduction committee of a union, even of a State union, need not be very large. It may even consist only of a single person. This person, however, must be a fine organizer, able to set many others at work. Moreover, he should be very prompt, for a little delay in acting might lose the society's hold upon some one. The committee will need to obtain the co-operation of the corresponding secretaries in all the societies, and should be very enthusiastic and systematic.

Advertising the Committee.—The success of the work of the introduction committee depends largely upon the degree in which it makes its work well known. Endeavorers everywhere should understand that all the unions, including the State union, have these introduction committees, eager to learn of the fact when an Endeavorer goes from one town to another, and eager to welcome the Endeavorer and place him at once in the midst of happy church and society surroundings. The State paper should often print a list of the introduction committees of the unions, with their addresses, and every corresponding secretary in the State should have a printed copy of this list. Advertise the committee and its work at the State conventions by speeches and reports, and also by printed lists of introduction committees and their addresses placed in the hands of all the delegates.

The Committee at Work.—When an Endeavorer goes from one place to another the corresponding secretary will at once communicate the fact to the introduction committee of the union in the place to which the Endeavorer has gone. Of course the president of the Endeavorer's society may do this, or the president of the union, or any one else, for that matter. If the Endeavorer's union has an introduction committee and that committee knows of the removal, the one committee will notify the other. Do not stand on ceremony ; it is better that several letters should be written than that the matter should be overlooked. If there is no introduction committee where the Endeavorer has gone, and perhaps no Christian Endeavor union, then you may correspond with the State introduction committee. Set some part of the Christian Endeavor machinery at work on the case. Do not let it go by default.

Next, the introduction committee of the place to which the Endeavorer has gone, having learned about him, will get to work. The letter will have told the Endeavorer's address and his denomination. Immediately the introduction committee will write (or telephone, if possible) to some leading worker in the society of the Endeavorer's denomination nearest to where he is living, and will give him the information. It will be the duty of this Endeavorer to look up the new-comer at once, bid him welcome, and do what he can to make him feel at home. Especially, he will tell him when the society meets, and invite him to be present and become a member. It will be much the best if the Endeavorer calls upon his new friend at the time of the society meeting (having first made the call of welcoming), and accompanies him to the meeting place. Put yourself in the place of the stranger. Remember how lonely he must feel, and how hard it must be for him to enter freely into religious work where he knows no one or very few. Try to make the transition easy for him, and you will win a good worker for your society and prevent his possible lapse into worldliness.

This having been done, a report will be made to the introduction committee, and this committee will report to the introduction committee of the union from which the Endeavorer came, or to whoever was the first correspondent. To save a worker to the kingdom of God is as great a work as to gain one. The business of our introduction committee is to save workers.

Boarding-House Bureaus.—The union introduction committee may run a boarding-house bureau, or this may become a cognate branch of the union work. Many Endeavorers go to a city with only a vague idea of where to find a safe and pleasant boarding-place. This important matter is decided for them largely by chance. They are likely to fall in with careless companions, and their whole lives may be ruined. Great good will be done if it becomes known that the introduction department of the Christian Endeavor union is in touch with safe places for room and board, and will introduce new-comers to these as well as to the churches and societies. If it is known that such a list of boarding-places is kept, applications for inclusion in the list will soon begin to come in. Each place should be investigated before it is accepted, and recommendations of some Christian Endeavorers well known to the introduction committee should be obtained in every case.

An Employment Bureau.—No union introduction committee can long do this work without meeting the necessity for becoming an employment bureau as well, though, of course, only on a very modest scale. Cases will be sure to arise of Endeavorers disappointed in obtaining the work which they expected to find. Sometimes these are cases of real need, and the introduction committee will be compelled by the ordinary principles of Christian brotherhood to come to the rescue.

Always, moreover, there is need in a city of finding work for those who are out of work, often through no fault of their own. If the introduction committee can introduce a willing worker to a job for which he is suited, it will surely be doing the King's business. This is work which the churches have not taken up or our unions, at least not on any extended scale, and it is work greatly needing to be done. To do it the introduction committee will need a knowledge of large employers of labor of many different kinds, and enough acquaintance with them to win attention to the committee's recommendation. This the committee can gain by the use of some friend or acquaintance, if it does not itself know the business man, for our Christian Endeavor unions have wide outreaches. Often the task of finding work for another is about the hardest kind of work imaginable, but the accomplishment of it will bring to the committee the warm approval of the Master Workman.

Friends, Anyway.—Whatever service the introduction committee can perform for the new-comer, it can perform the greatest of all services, the bestowal of friendship. That is what the stranger wants when he finds himself lonely in a new place. He wants some one that takes an interest in him, some one with whom he can discuss his plans, some one to whom he can relate his successes or his failures. You can add to his successes or help him out of his failures; but even if you could not, you can rejoice as he rejoices and weep as he weeps. In all of this let the introduction committee remember that it is winning the gratitude of Him who at the last day will remember to say, " I was a stranger, and ye took me in."

Class Work on Chapter XX

The Leader's Questions

What is the work of the introduction committee ?
How large should the committee be ?
How will the committee be advertised ?
What methods will the committee use ?
How will a boarding-house bureau be conducted ?
How will an employment bureau be conducted ?
How will the committee show its friendship for the
   strangers ?

Topic for a Talk or Essay

Entertaining Angels Unawares.

Subject for a Class Debate

Resolved, that our union should appoint an introduction
   committee.

CHAPTER XXI

UNION WORK FOR PRISONERS

Why Union Work for Prisoners?—A single society can do fine work for prisoners, and many societies have done it; but the work in any large prison is so great as to require all the societies of the union to do it in the best way. If many workers are combined, the work does not press too heavily upon any; but if only few undertake it, the overwhelming demands upon their time and sympathy and strength will be too much for them. Moreover, the needs of the prisoners are so many that the varied resources of different societies will be needed in the work.

The Organizing of the Work.—No work of any kind will be done till some one or some set of persons is made responsible for it. The union that decides to take up work for prisoners will appoint a prison committee, and will place at its head some one who is full of zeal for this work. The committee may well have upon it some member from each society, so as to interest every society in the work and obtain help from all. This member from each society may well form in his society a prison committee to work in connection with the union prison committee.

Starting the Work.—You will not undertake work for prisoners without obtaining first of all the hearty approval of the pastoral counsellor of the union, and therefore presumably of all the pastors of the union.

214

In the second place, you will consult the chaplain of the prison, within whose special field the prison committee will work. To gain his consent you will tell him something of what has been done in other prisons, and the fine results of the work there as reported from time to time in *The Christian Endeavor World*. You will also assure the chaplain that your only purpose is to work under his direction and to assist him in his heavy task. You will tell him just what you have in mind to do as suggested in the paragraphs below. You will declare that you wish to begin with one undertaking and see how it works out, and then go on slowly and surely from this undertaking to another till your whole programme is in operation, or at least as much of it as may prove to be wise. Then, having obtained the chaplain's cordial approval, you will go with him to the warden ; and you may be sure that your joint application will meet with success. In talking with the warden it will be well to quote the favorable opinion of some prison warden who has had experience of Christian Endeavor work for prisoners.

Become Acquainted.—Having obtained this consent of the authorities, the prison committee will take the first step in their great enterprise, which is to become acquainted with some of the prisoners—as many of them as possible. You can do this best if you approach them with some little gift, such as an interesting magazine or paper or book, or some flowering plant, if that is permitted, or some card bearing a beautiful and helpful picture and motto. This little gift gives an opening for conversation. If it is something to read, you can come again and ask how the prisoner has enjoyed it. It should be something you yourself have read, so that you can discuss it with him. It need not be anything religious, perhaps it would better not be at first; all you want at this stage is to become acquainted, to show that you are the friend of the prisoners and really want to help them. Of course in all this work the young men of the societies will visit the men prisoners and the young women of the societies will visit the women prisoners. Also, you will not set the younger Endeavorers to doing such work, but only the most mature in years, or, at any rate, in character.

The First Meeting.—Having become friends with the prisoners, or at least with many of them, the prison committee will get the consent of the chaplain and warden for the next step, which will be to hold in the prison a Christian Endeavor prayer meeting. You will talk this up beforehand among your prison friends, explaining the purpose of Christian Endeavor and the nature of the Christian Endeavor prayer meeting. Give a broad general invitation for all the inmates of the prison to attend, but do not have attendance made compulsory. Get a large number of the most earnest speakers and workers among the societies to come to this meeting prepared to take part. Use some topic that will be of interest and helpfulness to the prisoners, whether it is the regular Christian Endeavor topic or not. Carry on the meeting like an ordinary prayer meeting, with a large number of brief, warm, personal testimonies from all the Endeavorers present, with much bright singing in which the prisoners will join, and with many prayers. Do not ask the prisoners to take part; they are there only to see what a Christian Endeavor prayer meeting is like. At the close of the meeting the leader or the chairman of the prison committee will explain what Christian Endeavor is, will read the pledge, and will state that a Christian Endeavor society will be formed in the prison. Invite questions about the society from the prisoners, and answer them with the help and co-operation of the chaplain and warden, who will, of course, be prominent in the meeting. Then say that during the week you will call upon the prisoners one by one to talk over the matter and invite them to join. You will need the entire force of the committee to do this, spending considerable time in the prison; but this is a most critical period of the undertaking, and you will not begin till you can work out the plan with thoroughness.

The Prison Christian Endeavor Society.—Even if only a few prisoners give in their allegiance to the society at first, yet you will form the organization, sure that in time it will grow. Usually the prisoners are quite eager for it, as affording a break in the monotony of their lives; and for this reason you will need to be very strict in your explanation of the pledge, and try to weed out those that do not really want to get good from the society. At the same time you will bear in mind that if the greater part of the members are in earnest, they will be able to influence for good a minority that may not enter the society with the right motives.

The society will meet regularly once a week. It will take the usual Christian Endeavor topics, except when they are not so well fitted to the needs of the prisoners as others that may be substituted. Some of the prison committee will always be present at the meeting, and, if possible, the entire committee. They will take part just as the prisoners do, but will throw the entire management of the society into the hands of the prisoners—all the offices and committees. The prison committee will merely act as advisers. The enlargement of the society will be done mainly by the prison committee, who will have far better chances to talk it up among the prisoners than the lookout committee of the prison society is likely to have.

Work for the Prison Endeavorers.—The members of the prison committee will soon come to know the prison Endeavorers very intimately. They will talk over with them the work of the society, and will aid them with it. They will give them books and pamphlets on Christian Endeavor work, on the Quiet Hour, on the Bible, and whatever else will direct them in their work and inspire them in it. Especially, the prison committee will learn the chief trouble in the life of each of the prison Endeavorers, and will try to remove it. Is it worry about his family? You will do what you can to care for that family and relieve the prisoner's mind. Is it remorse for his past deeds? You will help him to right all the wrongs that can be righted, and you will lead him along the way of godly repentance. Is it doubt of God's goodness, of the salvation that Christ offers? You will work with Bible-born wisdom to show God's love and bring them to know Christ as their Saviour. In all this work you will soon need the help of your pastors and of the adult Christians in your churches. Before long you will see that this work will do more for you in the development of your powers even than it will do for the prisoners.

The Work of the Prison Endeavorers.—The prison committee will not do anything for the prison En-

deavorers that it can get the prison Endeavorers to do
for themselves, nor anything for the other prisoners
that it can lead the prison Endeavorers to do for them.
You will find it easy, for instance, to interest the prison
Endeavorers in the great work of missions, with its
splendid outreach and its abounding heroism. Out of
their very meagre resources they will be eager to give
for the support of the gospel. They will be greatly
pleased thus to reach out, beyond the narrow bounds of
the prison, over the wide world. The study of Christian citizenship will appeal to them, and you will find
many patriots among them. Bible-study will become a
passion to many of them, and they will pore over the
blessed Book by the hour, bringing forth some glorious
truths. As far as opportunity is given them to talk
with the other prisoners, they will be outspoken in
work for their salvation. In all this enterprise you will
have great faith in the possibilities of the prisoners.
You will come to realize that many of them have been
quite as much unfortunate as sinful, suffering from their
own misdeeds, of course, but also from the sins of their
parents and of society. You will cease to scorn them
and begin to pity them, trust their inherent manhood,
and by your trust you will draw out all their hidden
possibilities of good. And nothing will help the
prisoner more than getting him to help some one else
in the prison and some great cause outside of the prison.

A Word of Warning.—The prison committee must
remember that they are dealing with shrewd men, sinful men, men quick to seize upon every chance for
themselves. Some of them will try to " work " the
prison committee, and will enter the Christian Endeavor
society in the hope of gaining special privileges in the

prison and help after they leave prison. At every step
the committee will consult with the chaplain and the
warden, checking up their impressions with the wider
experiences of those officers, learning which of the
prisoners are to be trusted and which are probably not
sincere and are to be made to prove themselves in
ways that are more genuine than mere words.

Special Seasons in the Prison.—Christmas and
Thanksgiving, the great home festivals, give the prison
committee a fine chance with the prisoners, many of
whom are hungry for home. The Endeavorers of all
the societies will be enlisted in the work of providing
Christmas cards or Thanksgiving cards with beautifully
printed messages, or personal letters for the prisoners.
At Easter flowers may be sent to all the prisoners. On
the Fourth of July patriotic messages may be sent
them, and each may receive an American flag. New
Year's day gives a fine chance for pleas for the turning
over of a new leaf. All of these seasons will be utilized
by the prison committee and the co-operating Endeavorers.

When the Prisoners Are Discharged.—The most
critical time in all work for prisoners is the time of their
discharge. They go out into a world where everything
is fearfully hard for them. They may have been
soundly converted in the prison and may have hearts
set upon a Christian life, but they are distrusted on all
hands. They want to be industrious and to earn an
honest living, but they find most doors, sometimes all
doors, closed against them. At this stage the prison
committee must become an employment bureau. It
will not only sympathize with the discharged prisoners

and cheer them in their up-hill fight, but it will give them the practical help that they so greatly need. It will tell the Christian employers about the great need of the prisoners, and will appeal to them to give them work. Here the pastors will be of the greatest assistance, backing up the appeals of the prison committee with their own earnest recommendations.

Then, when work is obtained for the discharged prisoners,—any honest work, however humble,—the Endeavorers will stand by them, giving them the brotherly fellowship that will support them against the sneers, the suspicion, and the scorn that will make them outlaws among their fellow workers. A man can face the world if he has a friend, and the prison committee will try in each case to furnish that friend.

Of course, if a Prisoners' Aid society operates in your city, the prison committee will merely co-operate with it in its labors for discharged prisoners.

The work described in this chapter is the most arduous that a Christian can take up, but hundreds of Endeavorers have taken it up and have achieved glorious successes. What they have done you can do, and in it all you will have the glad approval and omnipotent aid of Him who will say at the last day to His obedient disciples, " I was in prison and ye came unto me."

Class Work on Chapter XXI

The Leader's Questions

Why should Christian Endeavor unions work for prisoners ?

How is prison work organized ?

How is the work started ?

How become acquainted with the prisoners ?

How conduct the opening Christian Endeavor meeting ?

How form the prison Christian Endeavor society ?

What work will the outside Endeavorers do for the prisoners ?

What work will the prison society do for the prisoners ?

How will the Endeavorers observe special seasons in the prison ?

What will the outside Endeavorers do to help discharged prisoners ?

Topic for a Talk or Essay

" In Prison, and Ye Came unto Me."

Subject for a Class Debate

Resolved, that our union should undertake definite work for prisoners.

CHAPTER XXII

UNION WORK FOR HOSPITALS

Opportunities for the Work.—Most communities now, especially in the more thickly settled portions of the country, have hospitals of one kind or another. In these institutions there is a great opportunity for religious work, but little work of the kind is done. Pastors visit the members of their own churches, but hesitate to seek out the members of other churches lest they appear to intrude. In the great public hospitals there is often the greatest religious destitution. Here is just the opportunity for an interdenominational religious organization like the Christian Endeavor union. It is a work too large for any one society, and requires the co-operation which is the heart of our union activity. Every union which has a hospital within its bounds should appoint a hospital committee, and set it to work uniting the societies for this blessed service.

The Hospital Committee.—The chairman of this committee should be some one with an earnest evangelistic spirit, who will enter into the work with a deep purpose to be spiritually helpful to these souls in sore trouble. He must also be a good executive, able to mass and direct the energies of many societies. Upon his committee should be some of musical ability, able to organize the musical talents of the societies for the hospital work; others of literary tendency, who will see to the papers, magazines, books; others of

223

practical nature, who will get together gifts of jellies and other good things to eat and drink; and still others who will be helpful in talking to the sick, cheering them up and pointing them to the Good Physician. The committee should not be so large as to be unwieldy—ten or twelve would be large enough,—but it should represent as well as possible the different sections of the city.

The Approval of the Authorities.—The first step in the work is, of course, to obtain the consent and hearty approval of the hospital authorities. Go right to the head of the hospital and explain fully what you hope to do. Take with you some mutual friend, if you are not known to the hospital head. Get some well-known and honored minister to go with you and emphasize your plea. Here is a place for the pastoral counsellor of the union. The hospital authorities will be reluctant to introduce anything that might be a disturbing element. You will need to be very modest in your requests at first. Ask only for a trial, the result to be carefully watched and official decision to be based upon the results obtained. Promise to be governed strictly by the directions of the authorities as to the time and manner of your work. Agree to use in the work only the most experienced and reliable of the Endeavorers. Present testimonies from other hospitals where a similar work has been found valuable. Do not be discouraged if at first you fail to get permission ; but continue your appeal for a trial, and you will succeed at last.

The Ministry of Song.—Perhaps the first work that may be done in hospitals is singing in the wards. For this purpose you will train a company of Endeavorers so that they can sing without accompaniment, speaking the words very distinctly and singing with good expression. They should be very familiar with the words. You will, of course, avoid sorrowful songs, such as songs about death, and you will choose the brightest, happiest, most cheerful songs you can find. Nothing is better for this purpose than the grand old hymns of the church, such as " Jesus, lover of my soul," " Rock of Ages," and " Nearer, my God, to Thee." Give the patients in the ward a chance to ask for their favorite hymns. Notice what songs they ask to have repeated, and learn from these requests what kinds of songs reach their hearts. Make this a ministry of good cheer and of uplift, of comfort and of hope.

Different societies may furnish the singers for different days of the week, if you are permitted to sing every day. Probably you will be allowed to sing only once a week, and in that case the societies will take turns. It may be best to form a company of hospital singers from the entire union.

Sing your songs not loudly, and yet brightly and with confidence. Sing with smiles on your faces and with joy in your voices. Pack the songs full of health as you sing them. The sick ones will soon come to look forward eagerly to your little concert, and the doctors and nurses will testify to the good you are doing.

The Ministry of Papers and Books.—Another work with which the hospital committee may well begin is that of gathering good reading matter for the sick folks, and taking it to them with cheery words of good will. Care should be exercised in selecting the books, magazines, and papers that are given out. See that whatever is presented is of the highest and purest character. See that the subjects treated are bright and hopeful, and that the results of the reading cannot be anything but good. There are certain papers and magazines and the books by certain writers that you can give out without examination, for they are sure to be helpful, but others you must read thoroughly yourself before you will be safe in distributing them. Divide among your committee this work of reading, and also the work of gathering the reading matter from the societies. The literature committees of the different societies will collect the reading matter, and a regular day in each month should be fixed on which the reading matter shall be brought to the headquarters of the committee. If any society fails to contribute, the hospital committee will investigate the omission.

It will be well to stamp each piece of reading matter: "Presented with the love and good wishes of the Hospital Committee of the Christian Endeavor Union." This stamp will lead to conversation about the union and its object, and it will be easy to turn such conversation to the subject of personal religion. Besides, you will have much religious matter in what you distribute; and you will have opportunities to talk with the patients about it, if you are wise and friendly.

The societies may be induced to paste many helpful clippings upon light sheets of cardboard easily handled by the invalids. Some of them may be pasted upon fans. One set of cards will be filled with bright jokes, another with interesting pictures for the little ones, others with poems, others with stories, others with facts about natural history, others with brief and pointed essays. The Juniors may make these for the children in the hospitals, while the older Endeavorers will make them for the adults.

The Ministry of the Spoken Word.—It is easy for the friendly to be helpful to the sick, but very hard for those that are self-centred. The head of the committee will know who are sympathetic among his committee, who are forgetful of self and able to put themselves into the places of others. Without the gift of imagination one can do far more harm than good in talking to the sick. Go to them with a bright smile, with a manly or womanly fellowship, with interesting news of the world, and, if the occasion is fitting, with uplifting thoughts of God and the spiritual life, and you will have no difficulty in making friends. Just a whiff of talk, for you will not be allowed to stay long. Nothing that could possibly be depressing. Only a bit of brightness, of jollity, of courage. It is very easy to give this when you get the knack of it. It is merely a little outgoing of the Christian life; but it will mean everything to your sick friend, and, though you will not realize it, it will mean everything to you.

Of course you will be happy if the conversation can turn easily and naturally to the one great theme of religion, but do not worry if it does not. You are known as a Christian Endeavorer. Your purpose in going to the hospital is known. Your helpfulness and sympathy will be standing arguments for your religion, even if you do not say a word. Remember, above all things, that the sick room is no place for debate. If the sick man is an unbeliever, you must set him to thinking all you can, but you must not set him to arguing. That would make him worse physically, and would not better him spiritually. Just let Jesus shine

out of your eyes and ring in your voice and glow in
your loving deeds. These are the proofs of Christianity that will at last break down his prejudice and
remove his misunderstandings.

Gifts to the Sick.—The nurses will tell you what you
may carry to the sick and what you may not bring.
Sometimes gifts of flowers will be allowed, and often
they will not be permitted. When they can be enjoyed by the patient no gift is more helpful, especially
if the sick one has no friend to give him flowers. Just
a few flowers, all of one kind, are better than a big,
confused bouquet. The societies will be led to bring
flowers from their home gardens at certain times each
week, and different members of the committee will be
delegated to take them to the hospitals. Many churches
will be glad to have the pulpit flowers used in this way,
especially if there are no sick of the congregation to
whom to send them. Attach to each set of flowers a
card on which is printed the statement that they are
the gift of the hospital committee of the Christian Endeavor union, and add a loving message in handwriting.

At Holiday Times.—It is at Thanksgiving and
Christmas that the poor sick people in the hospitals,
especially those without friends, feel their sorrows the
most, and it is then that the hospital committee should
be most active. Show the societies what a chance they
have of doing blessed work for the Master and of
sharing their good things with others. Little presents
for the inmates of the hospitals, if only a Christmas
card apiece, or a tender written greeting, will serve to
brighten the day and show them that they are not forgotten. Easter will be remembered in some way, and
New Year's Day and Mothers' Day.

Do Not Forget the Nurses.—The hospital committee will be working for the patients if now and then it remembers the nurses, and at the same time it will be cheering and winning a very noble set of workers. Many of the nurses are far from home and friends and many are quite alone in the world. Their tasks are very heavy and arduous, and any bit of cheer you can bring into their lives will be valued more than you can realize. The earnest workers on the committee will come to know the nurses very soon, and will form personal friendships among them that will be exceedingly helpful to both parties. Remember that nurses are kept from religious privileges even more than physicians, and the touch with vital religion that you can give them will be just what they need to keep their faith alive and active.

The Contagious Wards.—There will be parts of the hospital to which you will not be admitted—the contagious wards, and the bedsides of those on the danger list. But you will not forget these who so especially need your help. If you cannot go to them yourself, you can send them flowers and written messages of loving sympathy. Find out about them from the nurses as far as you can, and add to your messages a personal touch whenever it is possible.

Helping the Convalescents.—As the patients get ready to leave the hospital there is much that the committee can do. The patients may be worrying about the condition of affairs at home, and the Endeavorers can help remove their worries. This of itself will often make all the difference between continued sickness and recovery. If the patients are poor, those of the committee that have automobiles or can obtain

them from friends may arrange to take them home in
this easy way. The friendships formed in the hospital
should not be allowed to drop. The visits should be
continued till the recovery is complete. The influence
obtained should be exerted toward their joining the
church, if they are not already members. They should
be helped toward work, if they need work. In short,
these hospital ministries are only the beginning in
many cases of a warm, practical friendship that will
cause the erstwhile sick ones to bless the day that
brought them to the hospital.

Class Work on Chapter XXII

The Leader's Questions

When should an Endeavor union do hospital work ?
How will the hospital committee be made up ?
How will the approval of the hospital authorities be
    gained ?
What use of song will the committee make ?
How will the committee use papers and books ?
How will the committee workers talk to the patients ?
What gifts will the committee make to the sick ?
How will the committee use holiday seasons in its
    work ?
What will the committee do for the nurses ?
What will the committee do for the contagious wards ?
How will the committee help the convalescents ?

Topic for a Talk or Essay
" Sick, and Ye Visited Me."

Subject for a Class Debate
Resolved, that our union should organize work for the sick.

CHAPTER XXIII

OTHER WORK THAT UNIONS MAY DO

A Versatile Organization.—A Christian Endeavor union, which is to train young people for Christian work on a large scale, may undertake any kind of Christian work that is suitable for young people and that can be done by a union better than by the societies acting separately. This being the case, the scope of our unions is indefinite, and the work they may undertake varies greatly with the different circumstances of the unions and the varying abilities of the union leaders. Some of the more common and more important kinds of work have been described in the foregoing chapters. It remains to speak more briefly of a number of co-operative enterprises which unions carry on less frequently, but which they may well take up wherever there is a good opportunity.

Work for Foreigners.—If many foreign-born citizens are living in the city or region covered by the union, some work for them may well be organized as part of our Christian Endeavor training. A task well suited to the powers of young people is the establishing and maintaining of night schools for the teaching of English to these foreigners. They are all eager to learn English as a means of advancement in this country, and will gladly come to a free school for that purpose. There are simple text-books for the teaching of English that use many of the languages of the for-

231

eigners in America, but much progress may be made
by bright teachers without any text-book, but merely
with the use of objects and talk about them. The
main purpose of this work is, of course, to get close to
the foreigners and give them what is worth infinitely
more to them than the English language, a knowledge
of the Saviour of the world. Acquaintance with these
foreigners will soon show us many ways in which we
can give them practical help in their daily living, and
—as you will soon discover—they will be helping you
quite as much as you are helping them.

Work for Sailors.—Many unions situated on the sea-
shore, on the great lakes, and even on the large rivers,
keep up gospel meetings for the sailors, visiting the
ships regularly for that purpose, sometimes in launches
owned by the union. Systematic work is also done in
the furnishing of good reading matter. Acquaintances
are made among the sailors, and earnest Christian
letters follow them around the world. They are invited to attend the church services on shore, and are
given a cordial welcome in the Christian Endeavor
prayer meetings and socials. Sometimes Christian Endeavor societies are formed on board ship, and the union
forms special auxiliary Christian Endeavor societies of
the shore workers for the sailors.

Work for the Police.—This consists in the holding of
gospel meetings at police stations, the furnishing of
helpful reading matter to the stations, and sometimes
the forming of regular Christian Endeavor societies
among the members of " the force." Policemen are
largely debarred by their work from church privileges,
and will welcome the frank and manly Christian fel-

lowship of the Endeavorers. Of course this work should be inaugurated by some Christian policeman, and carried on under the close supervision of the police authorities. And of course, also, it is a work for the young men of the societies pre-eminently.

Work in Schools.—Hundreds of thousands of boys and girls attending our public schools are without any religious influence whatever. They come from homes that are careless or infidel or grossly ignorant. They can be reached through the public school and the acquaintances so easily formed there, and the Christian Endeavorers are the ones to do it. Christian Endeavor societies formed among public-school pupils according to the grades, especially in the older grades of the grammar schools and in the high schools, have met with decided success. The movement will gain in force and dignity if it is originated and carried on by the Christian Endeavor union, rather than by single societies. Leaders among the pupils should be approached, and should be made leaders in the work. If the school authorities consent, the meetings should be held in the school buildings themselves; otherwise in some private house or in some church.

Work for the Poor.—If the city has a group of associated charities, they will welcome the aid of the Endeavorers as visitors among the poor and as solicitors of money and supplies for them. If there are no organized charities in the city, there is double need for such charitable work as the Christian Endeavor union may do. Under the guidance of wise and experienced pastors the young men and young women of our societies may be a great blessing to many poor families, calling upon them in a friendly way and without any sign of patronizing them, learning their character and needs, and aiding them as best they can with their own means and what they can obtain from their church organizations and friends. There is no better aid, usually, than to find occupation for those able to work ; and if the union can form a free employment agency, it will set many a family on the road to self-respect and support.

Class Work on Chapter XXIII

The Leader's Questions

What work may Christian Endeavor unions do for foreigners ?

How may our unions aid the sailors ?

What Christian Endeavor work may be done for the police ?

Describe Christian Endeavor work in schools.

What work may our union do for the poor ?

What other general work for the community may our union undertake ?

Topic for a Talk or Essay

Our Union as a Force in the Community.

Subject for a Class Debate

Resolved, that our union should undertake some large new enterprise for the community.

CHAPTER XXIV

UNION COMMITTEE CONFERENCES

Why Committee Conferences?—No society committee, however bright and enterprising, can go far without learning the best methods of other committees. If the committee relies only upon its own ideas, it will run in a rut. One of the chief things the Christian Endeavor union does is to organize committee conferences. In these conferences workers along the same line from all the societies in the union meet and compare notes. They inspire one another with fresh zeal, they fill one another with new notions, they comfort one another with confession of failures, and show one another the way out of difficulties.

In the various chapters of this book dealing with the union committees—music, social, missionary, lookout, etc.—I have given suggestions for the holding of conferences of the same kinds of committees in the societies; but the societies have numerous committees not suitable for the union, and therefore a general chapter on union conferences is necessary, since we should have a conference every year, perhaps several conferences, for each kind of committee found among the societies of the union.

A Conference Evening.—One of the best plans for at least the introductory committee conference is to call all the members of all kinds of committees to meet in some church that has enough rooms so that each committee may have a meeting place. First, you will have a brief devotional service in the main auditorium of the church, with a brisk statement of the purpose of the evening. Then you will have the members of the different committees separate to their rooms, assigning to the largest rooms the committees most numerously represented in the societies. The committees will spend an hour in their conferences. At the opening of each committee conference the chairman will appoint some one to report the conference for three minutes to the main body, when all the committees come together again at the close of the hour. These reports will be lively, and will simply tell the best things said and the best plans proposed. Insist on the cutting out of all non-essentials, such as " So many good plans were given in my conference that it would take an hour to tell them all," and bid the reporters get right down to business with their first sentence and show how much they can pack into three minutes. Then close the evening with a short consecration service, and a social half-hour with light refreshments.

A Conference Committee.—The union conference committee will have general oversight of the union conferences. It will be the business of this committee to see that such conferences are held for all the committees represented in the societies of the union. If the chairman of the corresponding union committee will conduct the conference, the conference committee will merely serve as assistant, but will do whatever is required, such as seeing to the refreshments and scattering about among the conferences and making them go with a rush. If there is no union committee to take the lead, the conference committee will run the conference throughout.

A Table Conference.—If the members in attendance on the conference are comparatively few, nothing is better than a table conference. The Endeavorers are seated at a long table, clear around it, and each with a pencil and paper. The leader of the conference sits at the centre of the table and talks freely and informally, asking questions, inviting questions, and making the meeting a general conference or conversation. If the meeting can close with light refreshments, there is the table all ready! By using tables you facilitate note-taking, and also render the occasion much more fruitful of real discussion.

A Question Conference.—Any conference should have some programme, and the best programme is a set of questions or topics placed before the Endeavorers on the blackboard or a large sheet of paper, or duplicated or printed and placed in their hands. The questions or topics should be numbered, and the leader will probably invite the Endeavorers to call for any number they want treated first, and then next. Here are some questions on the different leading committees such as may be used in these conferences—not a complete set in any case, but specimen questions to which conference leaders will add other topics to meet local needs:

Prayer-Meeting Committee

1. What is the work of this committee ?
2. How long in advance should leaders be appointed ?
3. What is a leaderless meeting ?
4. What is a committee-led meeting ?

5. How is a dual leadership managed?
6. How can we get more prayers in the meeting?
7. How can we lead the Endeavorers to do more than read verses?
8. What are the gains of using questions?
9. How long should the prayer-meeting leader take?
10. What are the advantages of the pastor's five minutes?
11. What different ways of conducting the consecration meeting have you used?
12. How can we make the members more faithful to the consecration meeting?
13. What special forms of prayer meetings have you found helpful?
14. How can we avoid long speeches in the meetings?

Lookout Committee

1. What is the work of the lookout committee?
2. What is a good way to get persons interested in the society?
3. How can we make sure that candidates understand the pledge?
4. Who should join as associate members?
5. How can we change associate members into active members?
6. Who should be honorary members?
7. What use shall we make of honorary members?
8. How can we keep the pledge before our members?
9. How can we cause our members to realize their responsibilities?
10. How can we make the society more efficient?
11. When is an Intermediate society needed?
12. What is the advantage of a Senior society—one for adults?
13. How can we get the Endeavorers to take part in the midweek prayer meetings of the church?
14. How can we make the best use of the consecration meeting?

Missionary Committee

1. What should this committee do ?
2. How can we have interesting missionary meetings ?
3. How can we increase the money given for missions ?
4. How can we interest the Endeavorers in missionary reading ?
5. How can we get more prayers for missions ?
6. How can we have a mission-study class ?
7. What is a good plan for a missionary social ?
8. How can we give the impulse for missionary service ?
9. How may we gather and use missionary curios ?
10. What plan for a missionary meeting have you found effective ?
11. What aid should we give the denominational mission boards ?
12. How can we help city missions ?
13. Why should we push the Tenth Legion ?
14. What home-mission work can we do in our town ?

Social Committee

1. How may the work of the social committee help the society spiritually ?
2. How often should socials be held ?
3. How can we get every one present to take part in the socials ?
4. What part should refreshments play in our socials ?
5. What kinds of games are unfit for our socials ?
6. What is the best social you have lately attended ?
7. How can our socials elevate the amusement standard of the community ?
8. How often should we hold socials ?
9. How can we get large numbers to attend our socials ?

10. How can we make our socials instructive as well as interesting?
11. How can we get strangers to attend our socials?
12. How does the social and business-meeting combination work?
13. What are some good ways of beginning a social?
14. What are some good ways of ending a social?

Music Committee

1. Why should a society have a choir or chorus?
2. What are the advantages of a society orchestra?
3. How can we come to use the whole of our hymn-book?
4. How get the society to sing with expression?
5. How get all the members to sing?
6. How can we improve the singing in our societies?
7. How can the singers of our societies help outside work?
8. How can we interest the Endeavorers in worth-while music?
9. What use should we make of special music in our meetings?
10. Why should we not drill the society in singing during the prayer meeting?

Flower Committee

1. How can we take advantage of the home flowers of the Endeavorers?
2. How can we get money to buy flowers?
3. What are some good ways of decorating the pulpit?
4. What use shall we make of the flowers after we are through with them for the church?
5. How can we put personality into our gifts of flowers for the sick?
6. To whom that are not sick may we give flowers?
7. What can the flower committee do for the church-yard?

8. How can the society raise its own flowers ?
9. What besides flowers may we use to decorate with ?
10. What unique decorations have you seen recently ?

Press Committee

1. Why should every society have a press committee ?
2. Who should serve on the press committee ?
3. About what should the press committee write ?
4. For what papers should the press committee report ?
5. What are some of the qualities of a good news item ?
6. How can the press committee get these items accepted ?
7. How does the work of the press committee help the society and the church ?
8. What are some common mistakes made by news writers ?
9. How can we better the Christian Endeavor and church reporting of this town ?
10. For what periodicals of more than local range should we write ?

Temperance and Citizenship Committee

1. What are the advantages of a society temperance pledge ?
2. What temperance and civic studies should the societies make ?
3. What practical work for temperance and citizenship should our societies undertake ?
4. How can our societies instruct and train their young voters ?
5. How can we strengthen the prayer meetings that have temperance and citizenship topics ?
6. What civic work for our town can we do ?
7. What reforms besides the temperance reform need our aid ?

8. What work can we do with temperance posters?
9. How can we make Christian Endeavor count for the right in political campaigns?
10. How can we cultivate in our societies the spirit of patriotism?

Good-Literature Committee

1. How organize and conduct a reading club?
2. How bring good books to the attention of our Endeavorers?
3. Why should we have society libraries?
4. How can we improve the use of the public library?
5. What can we do to increase the circulation of religious papers?
6. How call attention to what is best in current periodicals?
7. How gather up the used reading matter of the community?
8. What use shall we make of the used reading matter thus gathered?
9. How can we better the literary taste of our members?
10. How can we connect our members' reading with the prayer meeting?

Sunday-School Committee

1. What are the duties of this committee?
2. How can we help to furnish substitute teachers?
3. How can we call attention to the Sunday-school lessons in our prayer meetings?
4. How can we help the Endeavorers to study their Sunday-school lessons?
5. What can we do to promote systematic Bible study?
6. What should the Sunday-school teachers do to promote Christian Endeavor?
7. How may the Sunday-school superintendents aid our societies?
8. How can we help in the Sunday-school concerts?

9. How can our different committees aid the Sunday school ?
10. How can we increase the number of Sunday-school pupils ?

Conference Speakers.—The committee conference is mainly for conferring, but thoughts will be stimulated by an opening talk along the line of the conference, provided it is a very brief one and very pointed. Do not seek a famous speaker, but a practical one. Get him to name his subject, or assign it to him. You may well ask him to speak on one of the questions suggested above for your conference. Advertise this opening talk when you announce the conference. Let the speaker hold himself ready to answer questions referred to him during the conference.

Conference Essays.—Brief essays may be used in our conferences, essays written by the Endeavorers themselves. Here again we must insist upon brevity—five minutes is the outside limit. The advantage of the essay is that some will take part in this way that could not or would not speak extemporaneously, and also the essay is likely to bring into the conference the fruit of a rather wide reading of books and papers.

Question-Boxes and Answer-Boxes.—These are both valuable adjuncts of committee conferences, provided they are well worked up. For the question-box the committee should see to it that some bright and worthwhile questions are placed in the box, and that the box is opened and the questions answered by a bright, brief, and practical speaker. For an answer-box some practical question is proposed in the announcement of the conference, preferably one that will bring out experiences and tried methods, and every one that comes is asked to bring a written answer to the question. These answers will be collected and digested in private by some good speaker, who will at the close of the conference give a summary of the best replies.

District Conferences.—Where the city union is too large for conferences including all the workers in the city engaged along a certain line, the city may be divided into districts and the workers will hold district conferences which will be conducted exactly like the union conferences described above. Only the committees found in all the societies will need thus to divide their conferences. Committees found less often, such as the press committee, can get together in a single conference.

Class Work on Chapter XXIV

The Leader's Questions

Why should a union hold committee conferences ?
How should a conference evening be managed ?
What is the work of a conference committee ?
How is a table conference conducted ?
What is a question conference ?
What topics should be added to any of the lists given ?
What use should be made of conference speakers ?
How will question-boxes and answer-boxes be used in the conferences ?
How are district conferences conducted ?

Topic for a Talk or Essay

The Value of the Conference Idea.

Subject for a Class Debate

Resolved, that we should have more conferences in our union.

CHAPTER XXV

PREPARING FOR AND UTILIZING A CONVENTION

The Plan of the Convention.—The first step in preparing for a convention is to decide what the convention is to accomplish. Every convention worth holding has a purpose—many purposes, doubtless, but one predominant purpose.

Let those at the head of the union consider what is the chief lack of the work. Is it the spirit of devotion? Then plan a convention breathing the spirit of prayer. Is it civic fervor? Then plan a convention that will be earnestly and practically patriotic. Is it evangelistic zeal? Then plan a soul-saving convention. Are the societies behindhand in the adoption of wideawake Christian Endeavor methods? Then plan a convention for the exhibition and advocacy of them. Upon your choice of a convention aim will depend your choice of speakers, the character of your advertising, and your emphasis all through the days of preparation. This, therefore, is the first thing to do—determine what the convention is to do.

Choosing the Speakers.—You cannot always obtain the speakers you would like best, but you can always try for them. Never give up the possibility of getting a speaker, however eminent, till you have made a trial. There may be some reason why the very speaker you think most inaccessible would be especially glad to speak in your State and at your convention. Pick out the speakers whom you think to be ideally the best, and invite them first. Do not rely wholly upon your own knowledge of speakers, but consult widely. A one-man programme will suit that one man and others just like him, but it will not have the breadth necessary to meet the needs of your wide constituency.

But do not, however famous a man may be, select one who is an egotist and who will speak merely to show himself off. Choose men and women of noble character, whose single aim is the advancement of the kingdom of God. They should all be sympathetic with Christian Endeavor, or at least not antagonistic to our society. Sometimes the observations made at our conventions have transformed an indifferent acquaintance of Christian Endeavor into an ardent friend of the work.

It is best to allow the speaker to choose his own subject, after you have carefully explained the part of the programme into which you wish him to fit. If the speaker is worth while, his own subject will be better for him than any you might present to him. In order to set him to thinking along the desired lines, however, it is well to suggest a subject to him, telling him that you present it only as a suggestion, and asking him either to adopt it or name a cognate theme.

Always remember that a speaker should be bigger than his subject; that is, the right speaker will influence more by what he is than even by what he says. Therefore you will seek primarily to obtain men whose spirits are in harmony with the purpose of the convention, sure that their words will also be in harmony.

Obtaining the Speakers.—Six months in advance of the convention is not too soon to begin the work of getting the speakers; indeed, it is often best to open correspondence with the principal speakers a year in advance. Usually the more worth while they are, the longer in advance is their time mortgaged.

Few unions can offer payment, but the speaker should be told that his expenses will be paid. If he is a very busy man, he will be far more likely to come if you tell him that he will be entertained at a hotel, for entertainment at a private house, however delightful, gives one little or no opportunity for work such as may be had at a hotel.

In writing to the person whom you would like for a speaker, tell him how many you expect to attend the convention (make a very conservative estimate), and just what time will be given him on the programme. Assure him that he will receive the full time, and will be introduced promptly. An experienced speaker has learned by many disagreeable happenings that this is not often the case, and he will be favorably inclined toward the invitation that recognizes this frequent fault and promises to avoid it.

In Touch with the Speakers.—If the speaker gives only a half promise, you will need to keep at him till you know definitely about the matter. If in the nature of things he cannot be sure of attending and still you wish to advertise him, state in the announcement merely that he has been invited and will attend if possible. If he promises to attend, yet you will keep in touch with him, making several excuses to send him letters of reminder—once to give him a preliminary printed notice of the convention, once to send him the printed programme, at other times to send him advertising matter in which his name appears, and finally, just before the convention, to ask him on what train he will arrive so that you may meet him at the station. Thus you will keep the speaker thinking about the convention, he will not make a conflicting engagement, and he will be preparing his address.

Paying the Speakers.—Some treasurers wait till the very last minute before his departure before paying the speaker's expenses. Others wait till his return home, thus putting him to the trouble of writing. Still others more courteously ask him as soon as he arrives what his expenses have been, and if double the sum will get him home without personal cost; then a check is made out at once, and given to him with a word of hearty appreciation. If payment is made in money (which is usually preferable to a check), a receipt will be made out for him to sign, so that the treasurer can present it to the auditor; even when a check is given, the use of a printed receipt is more businesslike, as the check may not be returned in time for the auditor's examination.

Entertaining the Speakers.—The entertainment committee, or whatever committee has charge of the entertainment of the speakers, should personally visit the hotel and see the rooms to be occupied by the speakers, noting their condition carefully. Do not send your speakers to rooms smelling of tobacco, without proper toilet facilities, noisy, poorly ventilated, hot, or otherwise uncomfortable. Look out more carefully for them than you would for yourself.

If they go to private houses, choose families where their comfort will be cared for, where they will be honored, but where they will not be bored with constant attention, but sometimes left to themselves. The richest families are not always the best hosts.

Meet the speakers at their trains, having found out beforehand what those trains are to be, and escort them to their lodgings. Tell them just how to reach the convention meeting-place, and, if it is at all difficult to find, send some one to go with them the first time. A bouquet of flowers placed in a speaker's room is a graceful attention, sure to be appreciated. Leave with him a copy of the convention programme, even if you have sent him one. Pin upon him at once the convention badge. He will be delighted to be met at the train by a group of Endeavorers singing and cheering, and, if possible, it is fine to send him off in the same lively fashion. Give him a ride around the city while he is with you, and show him its attractions. Some of the friends of Christian Endeavor will be glad to entertain him at their houses for special meals, even if he is at the hotel, but these should be persons whom you are sure he will be glad to meet. It requires only a little knowledge of human nature to be sure that speakers entertained in this cordial way will give their very best to the convention.

Advertising the Convention.—The convention poster is perhaps the first piece of convention advertising matter to be prepared. Some unique design, well drawn and well printed, will be of especial value. It should introduce the convention emblem, which should appear also on the badge and in the programme. This emblem may fittingly have to do with the convention city. If the town's chief industry is the manufacture of shoes, the convention emblem may be a tiny shoe. If the church which is the meeting-place has a conspicuous spire, this may be the convention emblem. If a river passing through the town has a well-known fall, that may become the pictorial designation of the convention.

These posters will be sent to all the societies, for placing on the walls of their meeting-rooms. Others will be sent to the unions, for posting in railway stations and other places. A circular will be carefully prepared setting forth the aims of the convention, the principal speakers and topics, the attractions of the convention city, and the advantages to be gained from attendance. Get every union to appoint an excursion manager, whose task it will be to get up the union delegation and pilot it to the convention. The names of these excursion managers will be printed on the circulars sent to their respective cities.

A little article about the convention will be printed and sent to all the newspapers in the State, including, of course, all the religious papers. You will follow this with convention news items from time to time, telling about the prominent speakers and the chief features of the coming gathering. Also other circulars will follow the first one sent to the societies, each circular adding to the information given in the preceding ones. Print some of these in poster form, for display in the society meeting-rooms.

The Convention Committee.—The central committee of the convention will consist of the usual officers, president, vice-president, secretary, and treasurer, with the chairmen of the convention sub-committees, those on printing and publicity, on decorations, music, Junior rally, registration, reception, entertainment, ushers, and finance. Each of these chairmen will have a committee under him, large or small according to the duty of the committee and the size of the convention. This committee should hold frequent meetings for discussion of all the important matters connected with the convention, and should, of course, be constantly in communication with the State officers, especially the president and field secretary.

As the time for the convention draws near, all the members of all the committees should meet, and rousing speakers should tell them just what their duties are to be during the coming days, and fill them full of zeal for their important work.

Financing the Convention.—The expenses of a State convention are for the programmes and badges, the expenses of speakers, the decorations, the advertising of the convention in advance, and sometimes for the convention meeting-place. They may be met by the societies entertaining the convention, without aid from outside. If the convention is a large one and the entertaining union is a small one, they may need to canvass the merchants of the place and others likely to be benefited by the convention, such as the street-car company. Churches also may be willing to make contributions. The work of gathering these subscriptions is the important task of the convention finance committee, which may well be the same as the finance committee of the entertaining union.

Sometimes the convention chorus, after long practice, gives a concert just before the convention, and the receipts often suffice to pay all the convention expenses, while the concert serves finely to advertise the coming gathering.

Prayer for the Convention.—Prayer preparation is even more important and necessary than money preparation. Long before the time for the convention the societies of the union that entertains it will be praying most earnestly for its success, and word will go out all over the State urgently requesting the State Endeavorers to offer up petitions for the success of the convention. In this request for prayer mention the special aims of the convention, and ask that the prayers shall include petitions for the success of the convention in these particulars.

Sending Delegates to the Convention.—An unselfish plan, very characteristic of Christian Endeavor, is that of sending delegates to the convention from the various societies and unions. Their expenses are borne by the bodies sending them, and the money is sometimes appropriated from the treasury and sometimes gathered by private subscription. The Endeavorer thus honored is some one high in the affection of the Endeavorers because of loyal service rendered to Christian Endeavor, and very often it is some devoted pastor whose attendance at the convention deepens his love for our society, while at the same time it greatly strengthens him for his task. To be sent as a delegate implies a responsibility to bring back to the society or the union an inspiring account of the convention and give it as widely as possible, thus spreading abroad the blessed convention influence. Many a life has been gloriously transformed because of receiving the gift of attendance at a Christian Endeavor convention.

Badges and Banners.—The convention badge need not be expensive. Much thought and brightness put into it will produce better results than much money without thought and brightness. A pleasing design full of meaning and a choice selection of colors are worth more than costly ornamentation.

The same is true of the decorations of the convention city and the convention church. Good taste and an abundance of enthusiasm will produce excellent results without the aid of professional decorators. Prepare original window displays telling something about Christian Endeavor. Make banners bearing Christian Endeavor mottoes, such as " For Christ and the Church," " One is your Master, even Christ, and all ye are brethren," and " Onward, Christian soldiers," and place these banners in conspicuous positions. Use liberally the regular Christian Endeavor flags and streamers of the Christian Endeavor red and white. Remember that the purpose of city decorations is twofold, to advertise the convention locally and to make the visiting Endeavorers understand that they are welcome. For these reasons much time and care should be lavished upon this important matter.

The Lodging Question.—Long before the convention (and yet not so long in advance that the arrangements made will be forgotten or necessarily changed by changed circumstances), the entertainment committee will canvass the community for lodging-places for the delegates. Where the convention is to be a small one, free entertainment may be obtained; but in most States the convention has become so large that free entertainment has had to be abandoned. The entertainment committee, however, fixes the lowest price that is reasonable, and seeks to find the best homes that are willing to receive and care for delegates with this compensation. These will be largely the homes of church people, and the religious motive will be appealed to to persuade many that would not otherwise open their houses to strangers. Of course the committee will not ask any families that it does not know to be respectable and kind, likely to care well for their guests, and to this end the committee should be made up of Endeavorers from all sections of the city, well acquainted with their own neighborhoods. A written statement regarding each family and what it will do should be retained in duplicate by the family and the committee, for ready reference and to avoid misunderstandings.

The Reception Committee.—This committee should consist of wide-awake Endeavorers, those that can be depended upon, quick-witted for all emergencies, tactful and cordial. These are fine qualities, but they are not hard to discover among Christian Endeavorers. Squads of the committee will be assigned to the different stations and steamboat wharves, and each squad will become thoroughly familiar with its duties in advance. Some easily seen mark will be worn by the members of the committee, white yachting caps with red-lettered bands, " Reception Committee," being especially favored. The committee will escort the delegates to the registration headquarters, where they will learn their lodging assignments, and then will take them to their convention homes and introduce them to their hostesses. If the committee can learn in advance on what trains the largest number of delegates will arrive, it is a charming attention to go out ten miles or so to meet them. On the train, travelling those ten miles, you can make acquaintances and give a lot of information and inspiration. For giving zest to the reception, Christian Endeavor cheers and songs are valuable, and the reception committee will have a bright supply of them which it will use vigorously.

Convention Automobiles.—Probably the reception committee cannot press into service enough automobiles to transport all the delegates in that swift and luxuriant fashion, but in almost any community there will be enough Christian Endeavor automobiles to carry the convention speakers to their hotels and other lodging-places, to take them to and from the convention hall, and to give them restful drives about the city and sur-rounding country. Automobile-owners will usually be glad to perform this service, and only need to be asked. The convention automobiles should be distinguished by Christian Endeavor banners.

The Work of Registration.—Sometimes the register-ing of delegates can be expeditiously accomplished at the railroad stations as the delegates arrive, but few railroads will give the station space necessary, and often it is quite as convenient for the registration to be made in a centrally located church, probably the convention church itself, with whose location the dele-gates are at once acquainted. Sometimes several churches are used in the various sections of the city to which the delegates are assigned. Sometimes the registering is done at the convention hotels.

Wherever the registration is made, it should be sim-plified as much as possible, so that the delegates may not be kept waiting a wearisome time, for they are all tired with their journeys. Have a good-sized force of workers, thoroughly drilled. Cut out all unnecessary red tape. Many convention registration cards call for too much information, information that will serve no possible use and is never called for after the convention. You will want the name and home address of each delegate, that you may reach him after the convention with announcements regarding the convention report and with other communications useful to the union and to him. You will also find it interesting, if not directly useful, to know from what societies the delegates come and the denomination of each society. Upon the registration card will also be placed the convention address of the delegate, so that his friends may find him. All these registration cards should be kept filed in the central registration bureau, though a duplicate of each card may well be retained at the original place of registering. The different registration booths should be in telephonic communication, and it should be easy for the chairman of the registration committee to discover at the end of each day just how many have been registered.

Placarding the Convention Churches.—There is no better advertisement of the convention than a large streamer on the convention church or on each of the convention churches, stating that the Christian Endeavor convention will meet there on such a day. Put this in position as early as possible. In front of each church will be placed, a day in advance, a big plain placard announcing the times of the meetings to be held there on the following day, with the general themes and the names of all the leading speakers. Such announcements will do much to spread the information about the convention, and will draw many into the audiences.

The Convention Ushers.—Much of the comfort of the delegates and the success of the meetings will de-

pend upon the corps of ushers. They will be well
drilled for their work by a tactful and enthusiastic
chairman. He will arrange for signals to be made,
perhaps from the back of the church, by a display of
large circles of cardboard of different colors meaning,
respectively, " Preserve silence," " Close the doors,"
" Open the doors," " Open the windows," " Close the
windows," " Less moving about," etc. A system of
calls by means of a shrill whistle may also be arranged
for emergencies. If the weather is very hot and some
one gets faint, the ushers will be instructed what to do
and where to take the affected person. During the
convention the ushers will have many an opportunity
for a quiet word for the Master, and they should be
earnest Christians. The same remark applies to every
member of the convention committees.

Of course the ushers will all wear some badge or
armlet or hat-band, which will distinguish them easily
and conspicuously.

Preparing the Music.—The convention music committee should be headed by a man of fine musical
ability, which he will hold strictly in the service of his
religion. Thus he will not allow the convention music
to become a medium for advertising, personal or otherwise, nor will he let the singing of the convention
degenerate into a singing-school. The music will be
educative by its inherent nobility. It will please, not
by catchy, trivial tunes, but by its strong appeal to all
that is best in the human heart.

The convention chorus will be as large as the convention platform can accommodate, and will be thoroughly
drilled, but not over-drilled. The zeal of the members
of the chorus will be stimulated by the concert which

they will give precedent to the convention. Do not allow encores, for thus the music will trench unwarrantably upon the other parts of the programme. At the same time do not allow the rest of the programme to steal time that should be spent in the singing which the Endeavorers love. See that an adequate collection of songs is in the hands of every delegate. If you wish to introduce some special piece to be sung over and over, let it be some anthem or other worth-while music which will repay the time spent upon it and make the convention really contribute to the musical education of the Endeavorers. While you will have perhaps in every session some fine solo, you will not permit such features to take the place of the hearty congregational singing for which Christian Endeavor conventions are deservedly famous.

The Children's Part.—Probably every State Christian Endeavor convention and most of the county and district conventions now have a session devoted to the children. No part of the convention programme requires longer drill and preparation than this. The Junior superintendent of the union entertaining the convention will early apportion the work among the different Junior societies, and will herself visit each of them and see that the society is practising faithfully. An attractive children's exercise may be presented, or some elaborate entertainment, if you have the material for it ; but if you lack this, do not hesitate to give simply an exhibit of ordinary Junior work at its best—the concert reciting of Scripture passages, perhaps with appropriate gestures in concert, the giving of recitations, the singing of songs by whole societies, symbolic marching, question-and-answer drills on Christian Endeavor facts, on missions, and on the Bible, a model Junior prayer meeting or missionary meeting or business meeting, and the like. At the close may come a bright illustrated talk to the children by some one who knows how to do it, a talk that will not merely interest the children but leave with them some uplifting thoughts.

The Convention Excursion.—One afternoon near the end of the sessions will prove a welcome rest and change if it is given up to recreation. The excursion may be arranged by railroad or steamboat to the most interesting point in the vicinity. Plan for Christian Endeavor speaking on the way and at the end of the outward trip. If the excursion is not feasible, you can surely have a field day full of athletic competitions of great interest, making the tests so easy that girls can take part in at least some of them, and even having events for the Juniors. To make a field day a success the various societies should be notified of it well in advance, and the chairman of the field-day committee should see to it by visiting and correspondence that a sufficient number of societies train for it to make it " go."

The Press Service.—Upon the work of the convention press committee depends most of the effect of the gathering in the outside world. This committee will notify the newspapers in advance of the convention, sending them press tickets which will admit their representatives at once to all sessions, and asking if they will have representatives in attendance. Visit the local papers in person and tell the editors about the convention, and, if necessary, about Christian Endeavor. Ask each for an editorial on the day of the opening of the convention, and for at least one editorial while the convention is in session. Ask them to detail their best reporters to cover the meetings. Suggest interviews with the leading speakers, and tell the editors something about them. Have a press-room where the reporters can get up their accounts of the convention on convention typewriters, with the chairman of the press committee at hand to give all needed information. Put the press-tables immediately in front of the speakers' platform, and place upon them a liberal supply of paper. Give each reporter a badge and programme. A member of the press committee will always be at hand, ready to give information about the speakers and concerning all points that may come up in the course of the sessions. Thank the newspapers not only in the convention resolutions, but by special letter after the convention is over.

Convention Greetings.—It is always pleasant and inspiring for one convention to receive greetings from another, and a little money is well spent in sending telegrams of cordial greeting to all important Christian Endeavor or allied conventions that are in session at the same time with you. A list of these may be found in *The Christian Endeavor World*. You will doubtless receive replies, and these should be read to the convention. If the other convention gets ahead of you, have your convention vote to send a reply.

Convention Summaries.—The union executive committee should appoint some one of its number (the convention press committee chairman will be too busy) to write a summary of the gathering, taking perhaps a thousand words, and have it printed in time for distribution to the delegates at the last session.   The delegates will be asked to have the account printed in their local papers, including their church and denominational papers.   This account should be by the brightest writer obtainable, and should treat whatever in the convention is unique and specially interesting and helpful.

Echo Meetings.—Urge the delegates to hold echo meetings when they return.   Even if a locality has only one Endeavorer who went to the convention, he can man an echo meeting all by himself.   The characteristic convention songs will be sung by the audience, and also by a quartette or chorus.   Convention decorations will be imitated.   The speakers will wear the convention badge.   If there are several speakers, they will divide among them the various features of the convention, so that the whole will be covered.   The reports will be given without reading from note-books, except now and then a brief quotation.   Put into the echo meeting all the enthusiasm of the original gathering, fill it full of practical plans, crown it with the spirit of consecration, and it will wonderfully multiply the convention influence.

Reporting Bands.—It is a fine plan for a group of delegates who attended the convention together to form on their return a reporting band, which will go about to the towns and churches not favored thus with delegates, and hold echo meetings there.   Practice in reporting the convention will give these speakers skill, and very soon their recital will be pronounced a great treat.   Such a band may go to the aid of a single delegate who feels too weak to be the only speaker at an echo meeting.

The Convention Report.—The final printed report of the convention, prepared usually by the recording secretary of the union, cannot come out too soon after the convention is over. Be energetic and persistent, and you will surprise and delight the Endeavorers with your promptness. The report will be read with double interest if it appears soon after the convention closes.

This report will be large or small, in proportion to the union's financial ability and the number of its members subscribing for it in advance. It will be popular quite in proportion as you are able to promise full reports of the convention addresses that have been the most popular, so that you will make special effort to have these taken down verbatim by reporters, or else to get the speakers to write them out in full. It is always best to have the speaker read the shorthand report, if one is relied upon, since sometimes the reporter will make absurd errors in carrying out his difficult task. Do not be over-ambitious and allow the report to saddle a debt upon the union, but get out only so large a report as you can reasonably expect to pay for from the receipts.

Class Work on Chapter XXV

The Leader's Questions

How is a convention plan formed ?

How are the convention speakers chosen ? How obtained ?

How will the officers keep in touch with the promised speakers ?

How will the speakers be paid ?   How entertained ?

How will the convention be advertised ?

Of what officers should the convention committee consist ?

How will the convention be financed ?

How will prayer for the convention be obtained ?

How will delegates be sent to the convention ?

Describe the use of convention badges and banners.

How will the convention lodging-places be obtained ?

Describe the work of the reception committee; registration committee ; ushers ; music committee ; press committee.

What will be the children's part in the convention ?

How will the convention be reported ?

Topic for a Talk or Essay

The Value of Christian Endeavor Conventions.

Subject for a Class Debate

Resolved, that the gains from Christian Endeavor conventions well warrant their cost.

CHAPTER XXVI

THE MANAGEMENT OF A CONVENTION

The Presiding Officer.—Whoever presides over a convention has much to do with its success or failure. He should be decisive and energetic, earnest and consecrated, bright and jolly. He has many chances of putting his own spirit into the convention, and should see that his own spirit is just what ought to go into the gathering.

The president of the union should not always preside, but should ask others to relieve him of that duty during some of the sessions. Thus he will introduce others to the work, and among them some notable discoveries may be made. Moreover, he will thus be enabled to get a view of the meetings which will cause him perhaps to make some changes for the better in the management of them. The other leading officers of the union may be asked to take the president's place on these occasions.

Unless the presiding officer is a remarkably ready speaker, it will be well for him to think over each part of the programme well in advance, planning the conduct of each and devising interesting introductions for the various speakers. The effect of many a speech has been greatly heightened by the right kind of introduction. The president cannot prepare too well for all parts of his important task.

Promptness.—Be prompt! When the time for starting comes, start! When the time for closing comes,

close! You can if you will. You may need to post-
pone or leave without attention some very important
matter; never mind, nothing is quite so important just
then as that the convention should move on time and
the Endeavorers should come to understand it. The
spirit of promptness quickly spreads from the presiding
officer; so does the spirit of dilatoriness.

Keep to the Programme.—Some presiding officers
are absolutely regardless in adding impromptu features
to the programme, which is almost invariably overcrowded already. They call upon this and that well-
known clergyman, they introduce important visitors
"for a few words," they call up some former president,
they even sandwich in an unexpected consecration
meeting or open parliament. In the meantime the
regular speakers are anxious, seeing the interest of
their audience slipping away from them, and the audience itself is cheated of much of the well-prepared
addresses which they came to hear. It should be the
rule to get through with the programme first, and then,
if there is time and the audience is still fresh, to add
these extra features, provided they are well worth adding. To do otherwise is to sin grievously against
courtesy and justice to the invited speakers.

The Devotional Exercises.—The devotional exercises
that open the convention and all its sessions should be
planned as carefully as any other part of the programme; indeed, with even more care than most other
parts. Tell each minister who is to conduct the devotional exercises just how much time he is to have, and
choose men for the work that can be trusted not to ex-
ceed that time. Some have been known to seize the

opportunity to make addresses of considerable length preliminary to the Bible-reading and prayer. No devotional service is likely to be more impressive or more thoroughly Christian Endeavor than a series of sentence prayers by the Endeavorers themselves. Sometimes you may have three or four brief prayers by members of the State executive committee. Sometimes you may call upon the Endeavorers present to repeat Bible verses. Sometimes you may have the audience sing a prayer hymn, or read it softly with bowed heads. Sometimes you may call upon one minister to read the Bible, another to comment upon what has been read, and a third to offer prayer.

It is very helpful to introduce a half-hour or a quarter-hour of prayer and praise in the very middle of a session. The theme will naturally be the theme of the session, and much will be gained from the change as well as from the participation of the audience. These periods should be led by the very best speakers.

The Addresses of Welcome.—It is well to hear three brief addresses of welcome, one from the local committee, one from one of the local pastors, and one from a representative of the city government. These should be very brief and right to the point. They give chances to recognize different elements in the community, and the speakers always have interesting things to say which bear on the comfort and pleasure of the delegates. Five minutes is usually long enough for an address of welcome and for the reply to all the addresses, which may well be made by the president of the State union speaking for the delegates. Twenty minutes devoted to these four opening addresses will leave ample time for the main address of the evening.

It pays to plan novel forms of welcome, such as a brief rhymed address spoken in concert by local Endeavorers, one representative from each society in the city, not omitting the Juniors. Or you may have a few words—a very few—from a number of ministers, one from each denomination in the city having Christian Endeavor societies.

Invited to the Platform.—If the platform has room for them, it is well to invite to sit there the pastors and their wives. The sight of the great throng of young Christians will do them good, and the Endeavorers themselves will be pleased by seeing the noble faces of their Christian leaders. This plan may be varied at the missionary session by calling to the platform, instead of the pastors, all the missionary workers present at the convention. If special branches of Christian Endeavor are discussed at any session, call to the platform those working especially along those lines, such as all the Junior superintendents, all the Intermediate superintendents, and all the chairmen of press committees. If any especially distinguished person is present, do not fail to place him upon the platform, if he will come.

The Business of the Convention.—Our Christian Endeavor conventions are primarily mass meetings, inspirational and instructive in their character, and not deliberative. They are not for the transaction of business. This, so far as relates to the State union, is done mainly in the sessions of the executive committee. The officers, however, must be elected by the convention, amendments to the State constitution must be explained and adopted when necessary, and a few other matters of business must be attended to. All of this should be done with great expedition, though not rail-roaded through. We must remember that many are present to whom such details are quite uninteresting, since they do not belong to the society.

Sometimes "cranks" appear in our conventions, each anxious to get before the Endeavorers with his special hobby. They generally have resolutions to offer, and plead for them very strenuously. To meet this possible emergency and many others, a business or resolutions committee will be appointed at the opening session by the president, all resolutions proposed and all other matters of suggested business to go automatically to this committee without debate. The committee will consider all such proposals, and will bring them before the convention if it seems wise.

Recognition of Other Organizations.—It is usually not expedient to make room upon the programme for "fraternal greetings" from other religious organizations, much as we should like to do so and heartily as we believe in brotherly co-operation. But our programmes are always very crowded, and the religious organizations that could properly be recognized in this way are legion. If a beginning were made, it would be impossible to know where to stop; therefore it is best not to make the beginning. When a representative of some other religious organization is given a regular place upon the programme it is of course another matter.

Open Parliaments.—An open parliament on some question on which the Endeavorers can speak readily, such as "What is the best thing your society has done this year?" is always a lively and profitable feature of a convention. It should be conducted by a speaker thoroughly familiar with the subject of the open parliament, very quick and bright, and at the same time sensible enough not to make a speech, but just to say enough to start the Endeavorers. He should have wit and decision in cutting short long-winded speakers and drawing out brief and pointed replies from the Endeavorers. Every Christian Endeavor convention may well have at least one open parliament, provided the audiences are not so large as to prevent the young people who take part from being heard.

Question-Boxes and Answer-Boxes.—For a question-box the delegates are asked to write out questions on any Christian Endeavor problem or general religious or moral problem upon which they really want light. These questions will be handed in a few hours in advance of the session at which the question-box will be "opened." They will be read by the person who is to conduct the exercise, and he will weed out those that he does not consider best to treat, carefully considering his replies to the others. These replies should be very concise and bright, so that the exercise will not take longer than the time allotted it, and yet all the questions will be answered. If there is time, opportunity may be given for oral questions, and some prefer to have the entire exercise conducted in that way, some brave man standing forth to answer any question propounded to him from the floor. This makes an especially brisk feature, good to liven up a programme.

The answer-box is the reverse of all this. A question of practical value is printed in the programme or announced at the opening session, and the Endeavorers are asked to write answers and hand them in by a certain time. These answers are given to a good speaker who will glean the best and read them to the convention, with his comments. The question for the answer-box will be such as the following : " What new work would you like to see our societies undertake this fall and winter?" The answer-box, it will be seen, does not differ from the open parliament except that the answers to the question are written.

The Convention Collections.—The best way of providing for the convention expenses that are not met by local arrangement is to charge twenty-five or fifty cents as a registration fee. For this the delegates will receive each a programme and a badge. Sometimes, however, it is thought best to receive convention offerings, and when this is done a forceful speaker will explain just for what purpose the money is asked. In some States the money for the work of the State union through the year is raised during the State convention, at least in part, and the delegates come prepared to tell what their societies will give for this purpose. It is not well to take the time of the convention for these statements. Simply announce that at the close of each meeting the State treasurer or some assistant will be at a certain table ready to receive and record the pledges for the State work. This puts the matter in writing, as it should be. The treasurer will make a brief statement in each meeting summing up the pledges and stating what is the deficiency, if there is any. Endeavorers ought not to need the motive of emulation to inspire them to give for their State Christian Endeavor union, and the union that relies upon auctioneer methods of raising its money needs to educate its members up to a better standard as soon as possible.

The Convention Music.—This has been discussed in a preceding chapter. Let us add the suggestion that the music of the convention should be such as to lead to better music in the societies when the Endeavorers return home. To that end, introduce only the simplest and most practical musical features. Especially look around the city and State and find the societies that are doing the best work musically, and get them to give little exhibits at the convention. One society may sing by itself. Another society may bring its orchestra. Another society may have a fine chorus or choir. Other societies may have good solo singers or players upon instruments. Some society may sing an antiphonal hymn or an echo hymn. Such an exhibit will be worth more to the practical work of the societies than the Hallelujah Chorus.

Work in the Endeavorers.—Whenever possible during the convention, get the Endeavorers to do things. Have them rise and salute the flag. Have them read a hymn in concert before singing. Have them give the Chautauqua salute. Have them shake their own hands toward a speaker, Chinese fashion. Have them say " Amen " in acceptance of some earnest statement. Introduce into every session some feature calling for the participation of the delegates, like an open parliament. Make this a typical Christian Endeavor convention, where all take part.

Model Meetings.—One way to bring in the Endeavorers is by a model meeting conducted by some society which has planned it carefully in advance. Its members will sit on the platform. It may be a model prayer meeting, or a model business meeting, or a model missionary meeting. Everything will be carried on as in a regular meeting, except that strict time limits will be observed. The demonstration will prove exceedingly helpful, especially if the latest and best methods are worked in.

Convention Dining-Halls.—If the convention meeting-place is too far from the lodging-places to allow the Endeavorers to return to them after the morning session, and if there are no good restaurants at hand, the ladies of some near-by church may be glad to earn some money and help on the work by conducting a convention dining-room. Food, excellent in quality and generous in amount, should be served at a reasonable price, and the entire arrangement should be announced on all the circulars of the convention. If possible, the hall should be large enough and the force of waiters sufficient to serve all the Endeavorers promptly at one sitting, leaving most of the noon period for other purposes.

Overflow Meetings.—Experience will tell the president when an overflow meeting may be called for, and he should always have that contingency in mind. An overflow meeting planned hastily is a dismal affair, but when it is carefully thought out in advance it may be an even greater success than the meeting from which it is an offshoot.

Much depends upon the leader. He is handling a more or less disappointed crowd, and he must know how to put it into a good humor and keep it there. The speakers may come from the main meeting, only in a different order, so as to admit of transporting them. There will be inevitable intervals which the leader will be prepared to fill in with singing and with little talks by himself and others. If an entirely different set of speakers is prepared for overflow meetings, the leader's course is simpler. Some of the State officers may be detailed for that duty; especially the ministers among them, who will be readier speakers. It should not be forgotten that the overflow crowd is not likely to be made up largely of Christian Endeavorers, and therefore the topics discussed should not be technical Christian Endeavor topics, but the meeting should be adapted to a general audience.

The Quiet Hour.—Most Christian Endeavor conventions lasting for more than one day provide for Quiet Hour sessions early in the morning, so that each day may start in the spirit of devotion. These Quiet Hour periods will be placed in charge of a man who is not only spiritual himself, but capable of arousing spiritual thoughts in others—which is a very different matter. If there is any other speaker he should have the same characteristics. The music should all be tender, thoughtful, and prayerful. Quiet must prevail, and the doors should be kept strictly closed during the prayers and talks. If you cannot get just the right speaker, it is always quite as well to hold a Christian Endeavor prayer meeting, or rather, a consecration meeting.

Convention Evangelism.—The Quiet Hours of the convention may well be made evangelistic, calls for decision for Christ being made at the close of each session. But every convention may well have its evangelistic committee, whose duty it will be to plan in advance for evangelistic meetings in as great number and of as great variety as the local conditions seem to allow. There will be outdoor meetings, shop meetings,

meetings in department stores, and meetings as a part of the convention itself. Noon meetings may be held for business men. In the convention you may have an evangelistic meeting for men, another for women, and another for children, all simultaneous.

Under the leadership of some experienced evangelist or pastor, the Endeavorers will join bands for evangelistic work of these different types. The noon hour is the best for most of these services, and the Endeavorers will join the bands very promptly after the close of the morning session—probably half an hour before it closes. Announcements will be made in advance at the different places where the meetings are to be held, so as to arouse a spirit of curiosity. There will be much bright singing, the reading and repeating of parts of the Bible, many earnest, brief prayers, and much testifying of the pointed, practical, earnest kind which Endeavorers know so well how to give. At the close there will always be the call for Christian decisions. The Endeavorers will be late for luncheon, and may have to go without luncheon altogether, but they will have done great good, and will have received an impetus for this blessed work which will lead many of them to take it up with their home societies.

The Bible-Study Period.—Many Christian Endeavor conventions set apart an hour a day for Bible study. When this is done, the work should be suggestive of what may be accomplished by the societies when the delegates return to them. It should be an exhibition of method rather than a course of lectures or series of recitations. If it is dry and formal, it will inspire a distaste for the Bible and for Bible study, and will thus defeat its own aims. Actual Bible study should be carried on, but only by way of illustration, only to show how the Endeavorers can study their Bibles to greater profit when they go home. If this aim is kept before the leader, his work will be most fruitful.

The School of Methods.—Practically all our Christian Endeavor conventions have well-developed schools of methods, a portion of each day set apart to the consideration of the freshest and best ways of doing things. Usually several sets of workers meet separately and simultaneously—the Junior superintendents, the Intermediate superintendents, sometimes the missionary workers, and always there is one section for the consideration of Christian Endeavor committee work of all kinds. These conferences take up numerous topics in turn, each being introduced by a bright and practical speaker, who is followed by a general discussion with questions. The whole is kept moving briskly by the leader, who may well be the State superintendent of Junior or Intermediate work, of missions, or of the other work under consideration. In these conferences the workers from different parts of the State find their best opportunity for the gathering and exchange of ideas. Ample time should be given them, and the full programme of each should be inserted in the convention programme. It is well to appoint for each conference a bright Christian Endeavor " reporter," who will tell at the next general session of the convention just the best points brought out in the conference he has attended. Each of these reports should be strictly limited to a minute—a mere whiff.

Denominational Rallies.—Once during a convention it is pleasant and profitable to gather the Endeavorers into groups, each denomination by itself. If the companies are large, their members are proud that they contribute so much to Christian Endeavor and are eager to add to their number. When the groups are small, their members seek to learn how they may interest more of the young people and pastors of their churches. In these gatherings the denominational secretaries and other leaders get close to their young people, and find many opportunities of starting practical work. Much is said to encourage loyalty to the denominations, while at the same time, as is inevitable in a Christian Endeavor gathering, the spirit of Christian union is néver absent.

County Rallies.—Similarly it is good for the En-deavorers from the different counties to meet briefly during a convention, that their county leaders may discuss with them the difficulties and hopes of the county unions, and that they may plan ways of reporting the convention throughout the counties and of doing advance work in the coming year. These county rallies need not occupy more than an hour, and they can be made very profitable, though only two Endeavorers, in some cases, get together.

The Convention Closes.—The closing session of the convention should be planned with a view to send the delegates home in a joyous mood, exalted to a high degree of purpose and of hope. Sometimes it is called a " purpose meeting " and sometimes a " consecration meeting," but the thought is the same. Often the convention ends with a strong sermon followed by a regular Christian Endeavor testimony meeting, the Endeavorers telling what new desire and determination the convention has put into their lives. Do not leave this most important of all the meetings too much to chance.   Plan for it carefully, and put your strongest speakers into it, and yet leave enough room in it for spontaneous expressions from the delegates.   Make it, to the young people themselves and to those present that are not members of our society, a glorious exhibition of the spirit of Christian Endeavor.

Class Work on Chapter XXVI

The Leader's Questions

How should the presiding officer of a convention do his work ?

What degree of promptness should be sought ?

How strictly should the presiding officer keep to the programme ?

Of what sort should the devotional exercises be ?

Describe the ideal address of welcome.

Who should be invited to the platform ?

How should the convention business be conducted ?

Describe a good convention open parliament; a question-box ; an answer-box.

What part should music play in the convention ?

Describe a convention model meeting ; Bible-study period ; school of methods.

How will overflow meetings be managed ?

How will convention evangelism be carried on ?

How will the convention close ?

Topic for a Talk or Essay

A Profitable Convention.

Subject for a Class Debate

Resolved, that a Christian Endeavor convention should be limited to strictly Christian Endeavor subjects.

CHAPTER XXVII

UNION PROGRAMMES

Tasteful Printing.—A convention programme need not cost much to be effective. Type is important, but ideas are more important. Colored ink is worth less than brilliancy of thought. The programme should be so printed that the plan of it stands out clearly and unmistakably, and when this is attained the less ornament the better. Firm, white paper, clear type, black ink, these are the essentials for a tasteful programme.

The best of printing is cheaper than cheap printing, at whatever price. The Christian Endeavor programme is to be an advertisement of Christian Endeavor; let it not by its fantastic appearance advertise a love for show or the spirit of exaggeration.

Suggestive Programmes.—In fine type and sometimes in neat borders many suggestive bits may be introduced into the printed programme. You may put there facts about the union and about the Christian Endeavor movement. Our motto may appear, and the Christian Endeavor pledge. An inspiring Bible text may be shown in some distinctive type, the text which is to be the keynote of the convention. Under the names of the principal speakers you may tell something about them, especially the positions they hold, the books they have written, anything to introduce them to the audience. Brief, pointed analyses of their addresses may also appear. A page of the programme may be occupied with snappy items about the work of the union

and its committees. The names of the union officers
and committees may well appear on every programme,
with their addresses. Pictures of the principal speakers
are often used, and sometimes a picture of the convention meeting-place, and scenes in the convention city.
Great pains should be taken to make the programme
worth preservation, packed full not only of the
temporary information regarding the convention, but
also of facts of permanent value to all the Endeavorers that will receive it. It should be made a
union document of prime importance.

The Programme's Interspaces.—Every programme,
except the very simplest programme for a single evening, should be carefully laid out as to time, the hour
and minute at which each speaker is to begin being set
down. Be equally careful to fix the time when each
speaker is to end! Usually the speaker takes every
second of time up to the programme time of the next
speaker, leaving no time for the introduction of that
speaker, for singing, or for the inevitable unexpected
announcements and other interruptions of programmes.
A good plan therefore is to designate the time limit of
each speaker in this way: 10:00—10:20. "Christian
Endeavor Growing and Going." *Rev. John Smith.*
Mr. Smith will then know that he is expected to stop
at 10:20 even if the next item on the programme is set
for 10:30. That ten minutes' leeway will prove the
salvation of the programme, very likely, keeping it up
to time, with the exhilaration that always comes from a
well-ordered performance.

Well-Knit Programmes.—A well-planned programme
will have a unity that will be very clear in the mind of

the person who framed it, and will become clear in the minds of the delegates as the programme develops, if not immediately. This does not at all mean that all the addresses shall have the same general theme, though that is sometimes helpful, especially for meetings of only one session; it means, however, that back of the programme is a well-thought-out purpose to do something for the societies of the union—to make them more zealous for Christian Endeavor, perhaps, or to lead them to use better methods of work, or to fill them with the spirit of devotion. Whatever it is, the programme will be bent that way, and the main addresses will have that object.

This thought is not to be insisted upon to the exclusion of the variety that may be needed in the work. Especially is a long programme of several days likely to become very monotonous if it centres too much upon one theme. The societies have many needs which such a programme ought to meet. Also we are to avoid in planning our programmes the artificial basing of them upon some word or phrase, such as "Trusting." For example, the following outline for an evening's addresses would be a poor one: "Trusting in Prayer," "Trusting in Money," "Trusting in the Bible"; because, though the topics look akin, they are akin only in the matter of that one word. Make your programme-harmony a thought-unity and a unity of purpose, and get whatever outward uniformity comes natural and easy.

Utilizing the Holidays.—If your union always has an Easter meeting, a Thanksgiving meeting, a Christmas or New Year's meeting, and a Fourth of July meeting, you will run in a deep rut; but the religious and patriotic holidays may well be observed once in a while by the union, if you can devise really helpful ways of doing it.   For instance, you might hold a midnight meeting on the last day of the old year, with impressive talks by the best speakers available.   You may have a star meeting at Christmas time, with five speakers, each pointing out one aspect of Christ's character, such as His wisdom, His power, His love, His humility, and His self-sacrifice.   These nouns may be printed on the points of a large five-pointed star placed before the audience.

Topics of the Times.—Sometimes the union programme can properly introduce matters of current interest.   If they have a religious aspect, and especially if they relate to any of the lines of work of the societies or the union, advantage may well be taken of the immediate interest in them.   For example, if the public have been reading in their newspapers about some great revival, the time would be ripe for a meeting of the union to discuss what the societies could do for soul-winning.   If a war is in progress, a peace meeting may be held.   If a prohibition amendment is before the people, you will hold a union temperance meeting.   Just before election you may hold a meeting for first voters, with instructions in the meaning of citizenship and the duties that accompany the suffrage.

Something Different.—It pays for a Christian Endeavor union sometimes to consider in its meetings a topic as far removed as possible from the ordinary, just to stir things up a bit.   Have a wise talk on the reading of biography.   Have an illustrated lecture on birds. Have a travel talk.   Have a debate, or an oratorical contest. Both of these plans are exceedingly valuable, and are seldom tried. These exterior themes are not to be used very often, of course, and never when they would take the place of some plainly needed subject; but, introduced with discretion, they serve to interest some in the union that might not otherwise be interested, and they freshen up the meetings wonderfully.

Pastors in the Programme.—While I believe there is too much of a tendency to fall back upon the overworked pastors for the speakers in our union programmes, and while I believe also that the fullest possible use should be made of the Endeavorers themselves, yet the pastors of the union are to be the union speakers very often. When an invitation is given to a pastor to speak it is well, if your programme admits of it, to ask him if he has some topic of practical interest to young people on which he would like to speak. An address is usually far more forcible if the subject is not imposed upon the speaker, but springs from his own observation and thinking. If you have some special aim for the programme, tell the pastor what it is and ask him to name a theme in harmony with it. It is often a good plan to have many pastors speak, giving each only five minutes. If they all take the same subject, you will have that subject enforced in many ways, and so firmly fixed in the minds of the Endeavorers that they will never forget its teachings.

Business in the Programme.—The business of the union, so far as it is necessary and wise to introduce it in a meeting to which the general public is invited, may be conducted so briskly and brightly and be made so fine an illustration of Christian Endeavor competence that it will interest even those who are not Endeavorers. Do away with long speeches on matters of detail. If officers are elected, and you want a speech from the new president, let it be a two-minute speech right from the heart. If an amendment to the constitution is to be voted on, have the reasons for it given with cannon-shot directness. If committee reports are to be made, boil out everything that is not interesting; the King's business is always interesting, but explanations of why it was not done are deadly dull. In short, spend as much time and thought in preparing the business part of the programme as any other part, and it will have as much popular acceptance as any other part.

Debates.—Once or twice a year introduce debates into the union programme. Any important religious or civic topic would be appropriate, any question of reform, any important question of the conduct of life. You may debate, for example, the wisdom of endowing churches, or mission boards, or newspapers. You may debate the value of trade unionism. You may debate the relative value of the prayer-meeting and lookout committees. Many subjects for debate may be derived from the topics named below, but the best debates spring from current interests, and the subjects therefore cannot be suggested here.

Music in the Programme.—Young people like to sing. Give them programmes bubbling over with song. They are not quite so enthusiastic in their listening to music, but some solo-singing will be enjoyed by them. If you have a union choir, as every union well may, yet regard every one present as a part of it and give them all a chance to sing. Look to the words of what you sing as well as the music. Uplifting words are set to as inspiring music as trifling words, and become just as popular if they once are given a chance. Do not be afraid to sing the same song over and over, and even the same stanza, till the music becomes familiar. Go back to it again at the close of the meeting and sing it once more. But you cannot safely do this unless the words and music are really worth while.

Prayer in the Programme.—If every Christian Endeavor programme needs much singing, so also does it need much prayer. There will be the opening prayer, asking for God's blessing on the meeting; but there will also be other prayers often, scattered through the meeting. Sometimes it is appropriate and very helpful to introduce a ten-minute period of intercession half-way through the programme of the morning or afternoon or evening. The address just before it will have led up to it, and the address following it will leap from it as from a spring-board. And for the close, every Christian Endeavor meeting most naturally ends with the laying of the whole matter before our Father in heaven.

Consecration-Meeting Topics.—Often it is helpful to close a convention or even a one-session union meeting with a consecration meeting. This meeting will, of course, emphasize the main theme of the convention or of the session, and therefore a list of subjects can be only suggestive, but the following topics will hint at the nature of these consecration services: " Christ in Our Work "; " Unselfish Labors for Christ and the Church "; " The Purpose and Power of Prayer ";

"What Are You Going to Do about It?" "Begin Now"; "The Trust That Never Falters"; "Bible Promises That Are Dear to Me"; "Hymns That Have Helped"; "A Purpose Meeting"; "Prayer for God's Guidance"; "Now What for the Coming Year?" "Getting a Future out of the Past."

Popularizing Christian Endeavor Methods.—One great aim of our union meetings is to arouse the societies to the need for some kind of Christian Endeavor work and give instructions for it. This work will often be something that has recently been introduced, and therefore examples cannot be given here; but often it will be wise to emphasize some of the stand-bys of Christian Endeavor, and you can do it with such subjects as the following:

THE PLEDGE.—"What the Pledge Can Do and What It Cannot Do"; "The Pledge, a Staff, not a Crutch"; "The Links of a Glorious Chain" (five-minute talks by a series of speakers, each taking a section of the pledge); "Power from the Pledge"; "Hindrances in Pledge-Keeping, and How to Overcome Them."

THE PRAYER MEETING.—"Prayer-Meeting Preparation"; "A Prayer Meeting That Counts"; "How to Enjoy the Prayer Meeting"; "Prayer-Meeting Perplexities"; "Prayer-Meeting Power"; "Little Things That Spoil Our Meetings"; "Making the Meeting Go"; "Leaders That Lead"; "What Is Committed to the Prayer-Meeting Committee"; "Sunday Prayers and Monday Cares."

THE LOOKOUT COMMITTEE.—"Look Out for New Members"; "Look Out for the Old Members"; "How to Make the Most of Associate Members"; "How to

Use the Honorary Members"; "How to Vitalize the Pledge"; "Looking Out for Society Defects"; "Lookouts with Their Eyes Shut"; "How Lookout-Committee Service Develops the Endeavorer."

THE MISSIONARY COMMITTEE.—" What Is a Good Missionary Meeting?" "Missionary Money and Men "; " Why the Tithe?" " How to Get Real Participation in the Missionary Meeting "; " Those Fascinating Books on Missions "; " The Why and the How of the Mission-Study Class."

THE SOCIAL COMMITTEE.—"Social to Save"; "What Games Shall We Play?" " Recreation That Really Recreates"; "How to Transplant the Wall Flower "; " Making Strangers Feel at Home "; " The Christianity of Calling"; " What Is a Genuine Christian Endeavor Social?"

THE MUSIC COMMITTEE.—" How to Sing a Hymn "; "What to Do with Those That Can Sing and Won't Sing "; "What Is Good Music?" "Getting the Devotional Spirit into Our Singing"; "Christian Endeavor Singing for Christ "; "How to Get Better Singing in Our Societies."

THE FLOWER COMMITTEE.—" A Fragrant Service "; "Using Flowers as Rewards "; " Christian Endeavor Gardeners "; " New Ideas in Decorations."

THE SUNDAY-SCHOOL COMMITTEE.—" Christian Endeavor Helping the Sunday School "; " The Sunday School Helping Christian Endeavor "; " Christian Endeavor at the Right Hand of the Sunday-School Superintendent."

THE GOOD-LITERATURE COMMITTEE.—" What is a Good Book?" " How Our Societies Can Cultivate the Taste for Good Reading "; " The Wise Use of Newspapers"; " The Dangers and Delights of Novel-

Reading "; "Push Good Periodicals "; " What to Do
with Used Reading-Matter."

THE TEMPERANCE AND CITIZENSHIP COMMIT-
TEE.—" A Society Temperance Pledge "; " How
Christian Endeavor Can Aid the Great Reforms ";
" Training in Citizenship "; " Work for a Better
Town "; " Purity and Power in Politics "; " A Citizen
Unafraid."

THE EXECUTIVE COMMITTEE.—" The Executive
Committee the Heart of the Society "; " A Model
Executive-Committee Meeting "; " How to Keep the
Society in Action "; " An Executive Committee That
Executes."

THE OFFICERS.—" A President That Presides ";
" The Greatly Needed Vice-President "; " The Record-
ing Secretary's Pen "; " Corresponding Secretaries
That Correspond "; " An Efficient Treasurer "; " The
Work of a Finance Committee "; " A Helpful Pianist."

THE JUNIOR SOCIETY.—" How to Help the Junior
Superintendent "; " Why a Junior Society in Your
Church ? " " The Work of a Junior Committee ";
" The Joy and Reward of Work with Children."

THE INTERMEDIATE SOCIETY.—" When Is an Intermediate Society Needed ? " " Junior, Intermediate,
Young People—a Splendid Trio."

OTHER CHRISTIAN ENDEAVOR ORGANIZATIONS.—
" Why Senior Societies ? " " Why Mothers' So-
cieties ? " " What Christian Endeavor Can Do for
Prisoners "; " Christian Endeavor on Ship-Board ";
" Office Christian Endeavor "; " Rural Christian En-
deavor "; "Family Christian Endeavor "; " Correspond-
ing Christian Endeavor Societies "; " The Tenth
Legion "; " Comrades of the Quiet Hour "; " The
Christian Endeavor Peace Union "; " Christian En-

deavor Life-Work Recruits "; " Christian Endeavor Experts."

PATRIOTIC TOPICS.—" The Fallacy of ' Our Country, Right or Wrong ' "; " What We Owe to Our Fatherland "; " Every American a Debtor to America "; " The Glory of Old Glory " (of course such topics will be framed suitably to the nation in which they are used) ; " False Patriots and True "; " Nationalism and Internationalism "; " Robert Ross, the Christian Endeavor Martyr."

TEMPERANCE THEMES.—" Liquor Laws and License "; " Progress and Prohibition "; " A Saloonless Nation "; " A Saloonless World "; " Disease-Spreading Saloons "; " The Strength of Total Abstinence "; " Fallacies of Moderate Drinking "; " Half-Way Temperance Measures and the Results "; " The Temperance Wave "; " A Seat on the Water Wagon."

" FOR THE CHURCH."—" The Coming Triumph of Christianity "; " Holding Up Our Pastor's Hands "; " Our Duty and Privilege in the Church Prayer Meeting "; " How to Have a Notable Sunday Evening Service "; " Why Join the Church ? " " How to Be a Worth-While Church Member "; " What We Joined When We Joined the Church."

SOUL-SAVING SUBJECTS.—" The Priceless Worth of a Single Soul "; " Eternity—What Does It Mean to You ? " " How to Talk Religion "; " Every Christian an Evangelist "; " Bible-Based Evangelism "; " How to Win Souls "; " Be Ye Fishers of Men "; " The Wise Soul-Winner "; " Stars in Your Crown "; " Soul-Winning—You Can if You Will "; " Are You Winning Your Associates ? "

THE MISSIONARY MOTIVE.—" The Wide Outreach of Our Religion "; " Into All the World "; " Beginning at Jerusalem"; "Heathen Here at Home"; "The Ever-Shifting Home-Mission Field"; "Home Missions around the Corner"; "Home Missions at Your Back Door"; "Go and Go-spel"; "Dollar and Duty"; "Missionary Christians and Missing Christians"; "Our Proxies, the Missionaries"; "Our Responsibility for the Mission Boards."

OUR DAILY LIFE.—"Christian Endeavor Sunshine"; "Christian Endeavor Grit"; "The Helping Hand—Is It Yours?" "Kindness That Conquers"; "The World Is Too Much with Us"; "Treason to Our King"; "Little Sins and Big Sorrows"; "The Mistakes of Youth and the Glories of Youth"; "Christian Endeavor on Week-Days"; "A Home in Which the Master Lives."

BIBLE THEMES.—"The Bible Library"; "How to Get the Most out of the Bible"; "To Read the Bible Every Day"; "The Man of One Book"; "The Splendors of Holy Writ"; "The Man of Our Counsel"; "Ever-New Light out of the Old Book"; "The Deathless Book"; "Bible-Reading and Bible Living."

THE SABBATH.—"Modern Inroads upon the Sabbath"; "Sabbath-Keeping and Strength"; "A Sabbath Day's Journey"; "The Puritan Sabbath and Prosperity"; "What Is the Heart of the Sabbath?" "Christian Endeavor a Sabbath-Defence Society"; "A Sabbath Well Spent."

EXALTING CHRIST.—"My Lord and Saviour Jesus Christ"; "Christ the King of the Ages"; "How to Add to Christ's Happiness"; "Ye Are My Friends if ——"; "For Christ"; "What is a Christian?" "Trusting in the Lord Jesus Christ for Strength"; "I Will Come in to You and Sup with You"; "The Indwelling Christ"; "The Empowering Christ"; "Jesus, My Friend."

Class Work on Chapter XXVII

The Leader's Questions

What part does printing play in a union programme?

What helpful general suggestions may be given in a programme?

How avoid an overcrowded programme?

How make a programme a unity?

How introduce topics of the times?

How utilize the pastors in the programmes?

What part should prayer have in a convention programme?

How popularize Christian Endeavor methods by our programmes?

Topic for a Talk or Essay

An Ideal Christian Endeavor Programme.

Subject for a Class Debate

Resolved, that a programme on one central theme is preferable to a programme with a variety of topics.

CHAPTER XXVIII

AN EFFICIENT UNION

Why Union Standards of Efficiency?—The Christian Endeavor union is a complex thing, as this book makes plainly evident. Moreover, our unions vary greatly, no two unions doing precisely the same kinds of work. It is impossible to set up standards of efficiency for Christian Endeavor unions that will fully picture the ideal to be set before every union.

And yet it is possible to lay down essentials for our union work, standards of excellence which are to be attained if a union is to be regarded as meeting its responsibilities. These standards will deal with the activities of the average Christian Endeavor union, and those which the average union may well undertake in addition to the work in which it is now engaged. Such a picture should prove an incentive to every union. It affords a means of determining the actual condition of the union, and sets before it goals for its achievement. All of this, if it is properly flexible, is well worth while. The portrait of the ideal Christian Endeavor union which is given here is presented with this purpose in view.

Take Your Union Rating.—In starting on the use of these efficiency standards you will need to know just what your union has already attained. Let the executive committee consider the standards, one after the other. If the standard has already been well reached, the full per cent for that standard will be credited; if it has been reached only partly, the committee will estimate fairly the degree of success attained. For example, if you hold two union mass meetings during the year, but do not often treat definite Christian Endeavor topics, or introduce open parliaments, or call upon representatives of the societies, or consider the Efficiency Campaign in connection with the meetings, you may credit to the union four per cent of the eight per cent which the standard calls for. Add up the per cents thus obtained, and you will find what part of the 100-per-cent total may properly be claimed by your union at the start. Then set out vigorously to raise to 100 per cent the union's 30 per cent, or 50 per cent, or 70 per cent, or whatever it is.

How to Start a Union Efficiency Campaign.—After the union executive committee has taken the rating of the union and formed its plans for the campaign, it will call a mass meeting of the union. At this meeting, first the union standards will be read, and explained, so far as they need explanation. Then a statement will be made of the union's rating and of the process by which it was obtained. Then the president, or some other officer, will announce what portions of the standards that have not yet been reached the union officers desire to seek first. You will not take up so many new lines of work as to confuse the union, but just what you can reasonably expect to accomplish within the next few months and with the force available. Having done this, you will go on to other points. But do not, either, undertake too little. Set before you enough goals to occupy the energies of all the union committees and of all the active members of the union. After this statement, call upon some of the leading society presidents to give their opinions of the plan, having previously told them that they would be called upon. Throw the meeting open for expressions of opinion from all, and close with a very earnest meeting of consecration to the novel enterprise.

Changing the Standards.—Most of the standards given below are those that all Christian Endeavor unions have at least begun upon, but some of the standards are not applicable to all unions. One of these is No. 12. Only unions near some large body of water can do very much work for the sailors. Other unions will substitute for this standard some different kind of work, such as one of the enterprises suggested under No. 14, or the conduct of a village improvement society, or of a public playground. No. 13 does not apply to the few unions situated where there are no public institutions, and other work must be put in place of this also. No. 22, prison work, can be taken up only by unions near a prison or jail; but most unions, alas! are so situated. Every union, however, is to feel free to remodel this schedule as it thinks best, keeping in mind the wisdom of a variety in work and of holding the standard high. This is merely one ideal out of many. The essential thing is to set up some worthy and definite ideal, and then strive toward it with all your might.

Dividing the Work.—Twenty-eight standards will seem formidable when you look at them in the bulk, but the difficulty vanishes when you see how many committees the union has and how many efficient workers among whom the work may be divided. In fact, nearly all of the standards will at once be assigned to union committees already existing or committees that you should form. The standards merely give the committees something definite and progressive to do. And you are to bear in mind that not all the standards are to be taken up at once, only those for which you have force, and those which appear to meet the present needs of the union. One step, and then another, goes a long way.

Recording Union Progress.—A union thermometer is an excellent way to record the progress of the union in this Efficiency Campaign. Draw an enormous thermometer on a large sheet of paper, made by pasting together many sheets of manilla paper. Mark on the right-hand side one hundred degrees. Mark on the left-hand side of the thermometer the schedule of standards given below (with such changes as you may decide to make, if any); that is, you will place at the head, opposite the first eight degrees, the words, " Executive Committee," or " Congress," if you use that term. Bracket the first eight degrees, showing to which standard they belong. So continue, till all the twenty-eight standards are set down. Paste black paper in the tube of the thermometer, adding more with each degree of union progress. You will be able to run up the mercury twenty or thirty degrees at least, at the very start. When any standard has been attained and the mercury has risen over the proper number of degrees, print the name of that standard opposite the degrees on the right-hand side and bracket the proper number of degrees. At the same time you may mark with a red underscore, or in some other way, the same standard on the left-hand side, showing that it has been attained.

Celebrating Union Advances.—Each step in the upward movement of the thermometer will be noted with joy in the union meeting, but after you have attained one hundred degrees you should hold a meeting of praise and purpose, gratitude for the work done and the new efficiency gained, and purpose to maintain the position you have reached and to reach even a higher position. You may well make up the programme of the meeting by giving five minutes to each committee chairman or officer in charge of a branch of the campaign, who will tell how the work was done and what results thus far may be noted. The closing address will be of congratulation for the past and exhortation to further advance in the future. It may well be by some pastor, and it will be followed by a consecration meeting in which the members of the union will pledge themselves to greater zeal and will suggest still farther advance steps which the union may make.

Here now are the

STANDARDS FOR A CHRISTIAN ENDEAVOR UNION EFFICIENCY CAMPAIGN

1. The Executive Committee or Congress.—Regular meetings, not fewer than six a year. Average attendance of seventy-five per cent of the officers, and, if you have the congress plan, of fifty per cent of the society presidents and other society representatives. [4%, to be counted at the end of four meetings.] At each meeting some definite work to be laid out for each committee of the union for the coming month. [4%, to be counted at the end of four months.]   8%.

2. The Mass Meetings.—At least two union mass meetings to be held during the year. Definite Christian Endeavor topics to be treated. Frequent open parliaments to be introduced. Representatives of the societies to speak often. Subjects of the meetings to be harmonious with the Efficiency Campaign. [Per cent to be counted when two meetings have been held.] 8%.

3. The Attendance.—An average representation of three-fourths of all the societies in the union at the mass meetings. [3%, to be counted after three meetings.] An average attendance of at least one-fourth of the total membership of the union, not counting those present that are not Endeavorers. [3%, to be counted after three meetings.] 6%.

4. Committee Conferences.—One conference a year to be held for each committee found in the local societies. The conference to occupy an evening, and to be addressed by an expert in the work of that committee, followed by discussion. [To be counted after one conference for each committee has been held or definitely arranged for. These conferences may be simultaneous.] 6%.

5. New Societies.—A definite effort to be made by the union lookout committee to plant a Young People's society of Christian Endeavor, a Junior society, an Intermediate society, and a Senior society in every church where there is a chance of acceptance. This effort to include personal interviews with pastors, the use of United Society literature, and correspondence with United Society officers for the removal of misunderstandings. [4%, to be counted after each church has been approached.] The increase of the number of societies in the union by 10% a year. [3%, to be counted after one year's increase has been made.] 7%.

6. Finances.—A union budget to be formed at the beginning of the year and definitely brought before the societies with a request for contributions. [1%, counted after the budget is presented.] Societies that do not send in their pledges to be visited personally by the treasurer or some member of the finance committee. [1%, counted after the first visit to all the societies.] Every society making some contribution to the union treasury. [2%, counted after each society has contributed once.] 4%.

7. *Officers' Visitation.*—A definite schedule to be formed for the visitation of the societies by the officers of the union and the committee chairmen, aided by the committee members, each trying to interest the societies in the branch of union work committed to his care. [Counted when the plan has been in operation three months.] 3%.

8. *Christian Endeavor Helps.*—The union to have a United Society Committee, to act as agents for *The Christian Endeavor World* and the many helpful books and pamphlets published by the United Society. This committee to visit the societies with samples, urge the use of these helps, and take orders, except when the society has such an agent. [2% when the committee is appointed, 4% when it has visited all the societies once.] 6%.

9. *Reports.*—Full annual reports to be received from all the societies by the union secretary. [1%, after the first meeting at which this is true.] Written reports to be rendered by all the union officers and committees at each executive committee or congress meeting. [1%, counted after three such meetings.] 2%.

10. *Pastoral Counsellor.*—The union to have a pastoral counsellor, to represent the pastors on the executive committee. His advice to be obtained on all important matters. His aid to be gained in presenting the society to churches and pastors that have not yet

adopted it.   [Counted after the pastoral counsellor has accepted the post.]   2%.

11.   Junior and Intermediate Work.—This work to be promoted by union superintendents, aided by strong committees.   [1%, after superintendents and committees have been appointed.]   Conferences of Junior and Intermediate workers to be held at least four times a year, and a Junior and Intermediate rally once a year. [2%, counted after two conferences and one rally, the other conferences being definitely planned.]   3%.

12.   Floating Work.—If the union is on or near any body of water traversed by ships, a Floating committee to be formed, to lead the societies in work for the sailors.   Meetings to be held on boat and on shore, socials to be given the sailors, literature to be distributed among them, correspondence to follow them up when practicable.   [Counted when the work is set on foot.   If the work is not practicable, substitute some other.]   2%.

13.   Institutions.—The lookout committee to seek to organize Christian Endeavor societies or conduct regular services in public institutions, such as old ladies' homes, poorhouses, and asylums.   These societies to be aided in every way after they are formed. [Counted after the work in some institution is well begun.]   2%.

14.   Philanthropies.—The union to undertake at least one form of philanthropic work, such as the giving of country weeks, the conduct of a flower and fruit mission, fresh-air work, the establishment of a free labor bureau, the organization and distribution of charity.   [Counted after one such work is started.]   3%.

15.   Good Literature.—The union to establish a

good-literature exchange, for the collection from the societies of good books and periodicals, and sending them where they will be put to good use. [Counted when the exchange is established.] 2%.

16. Bulletin.—A union bulletin to be printed, if only on a manifolder, and sent to every society or to every Endeavorer in the union. Three times a year is suggested as the right frequency. The bulletins will give in bright, condensed form just the facts about the union work that every Endeavorer should know. [Count the per cent with the second number.] 2%.

17. Efficiency Campaign.—An Efficiency Campaign committee to be formed, to visit each society and explain the Campaign, introducing the sets of Efficiency Tests, and setting the Campaign on foot. [Count 1% when the committee is formed.] This committee to organize and conduct at least one class a year for training "Christian Endeavor Experts." [2% when the class begins to meet.] 3%.

18. Intersociety Visitation.—A schedule to be formed in accordance with which each society will send a delegate every prayer-meeting night to some other society until all the societies have been visited by each society. The delegates to speak at the society visited, and to report to their own society all the good ideas gained. [Count when the plan is put into operation.] 3%.

19. Quiet-Hour Work.—The union to have a Quiet-Hour committee of one or more, to visit each society for the promotion of the Quiet Hour, and the addition of new Comrades of the Quiet Hour to the United Society list. [Count when the committee begins its visits.] 2%.

20. Tenth Legion Work.—The union to have a

Tenth Legion committee of one or more, to visit each society for the promotion of the Tenth Legion, and the addition of new tithe-payers to the United Society enrolment. [Count when the committee begins work.] 2%.

21. Civic and Temperance Work.—A citizenship committee to be formed for the promotion of pledge-signing, temperance campaigns, civic-study classes, and all other good-citizenship work. The committee to see that similar committees are formed in all the societies, and that the meetings on temperance and civic topics are well conducted. [Count when the committee begins work.] 3%.

22. Prison Work.—A prison committee to be formed, for the purpose of organizing a Prison Christian Endeavor society, if that is feasible; and in any event, of organizing the Endeavorers for doing evangelistic work in all prisons and jails that are accessible. [Count when the committee begins work.] 3%.

23. Evangelistic Work.—A union evangelistic committee to be formed, for the promotion of study classes in personal work in the societies, and the formation in the societies of personal workers' bands. [Count 2% when the committee begins work.] These bands to be formed in at least one-fourth of the societies. [Count 1% when this has been attained.] 3%.

24. Bible Study.—Where the pastoral counsellor approves, a union Bible-study course to be held during part of the year, for inspiration in the personal devotional use of the Bible, and for the training of Christian workers and Sunday-school teachers. [Count when the course opens. If the work is not feasible, substitute something else.] 3%.

25. Missionary Studies.—The union missionary committee to form a union normal class for the training of leaders for the mission-study classes of the local societies. One text-book a year to be taken up, or two, one home and one foreign. [Count when the class is formed.] 3%.

26. *Social Work.*—The union social committee to hold at least two union socials of various kinds during the year. One of these may be an outdoor excursion. One of them may be a union entertainment. The work of establishing playgrounds for the children to be carried on, if there is need for it in your community. [Count when the socials are held.] 3%.

27. *Music.*—A union chorus to be formed, which will hold regular meetings for practice as frequently as is necessary, and will aid in the union meetings. [Count when the chorus begins its work.] 3%.

28. *Press Work.*—A union press committee to be formed, which will establish branches in each society, and will supply Christian Endeavor news regularly to the local papers, sending the most interesting and important news also to the denominational and Christian Endeavor papers. [Count when the committee begins its work.] 3%.

Class Work on Chapter XXVIII

The Leader's Questions

Why should we set up standards of union efficiency ?
How is a union rating to be taken ?
How start a union Efficiency Campaign ?
How far may a union change the standards ?
How divide the work of the Efficiency Campaign ?

How record the progress of the union in the campaign ?
How celebrate the conclusion of the campaign ?
Which of the Efficiency Standards for unions seem to
you to be most important ?

Topic for a Talk or Essay

The Value of Standards.

Subject for a Class Debate

Resolved, that our union should embark on an Efficiency
Campaign.

Index

www.ingramcontent.com/pod-product-compliance
Lightning Source LLC
LaVergne TN
LVHW090045090426
835511LV00030B/118